TH.
MOGGERHANGER
CHRONICLES

MINISTRY AND COMMUNITY
VISION
Volume 1   1993 – 2004

PERSONAL REFLECTIONS FROM
CLIFFORD AND MONICA HILL

Other parts covering the period until 2015
when we moved away plus any later action
will appear in another volume

British Library Cataloguing in Publication Data:
a catalogue record for this publication
is available from the British Library

ISBN   978-1-912052-89-9

© Handsel Press 2024

Typeset in 11.5pt Minion Pro by the Handsel Press
at Haddington, Scotland

Cover image by Anthony Whelan

Printed by Helix Binders, Grangemouth

CONTENTS

PREFACE

Even before we finally moved away from Moggerhanger House in 2015 after 22 years of close involvement, we had realised that the story behind our purchase and occupancy as a charity back in 1993 and the years of prayer leading up to it, would be of interest not just to those involved at the time, but for posterity. We had not anticipated being stewards of a Grade 1 listed building, the architecture of which would be valued by the nation for years to come. When God chose Moggerhanger for us, we had just needed a base for the 'transformation of society' ministries in which we were currently engaged. But the Lord provided us with Moggerhanger House.

The digital age was in its infancy in the early 90s and we had amassed copious hard copy material in our records, much of which we left behind when we moved as we hoped it would be of value, but we had retained a number of items of relevant importance. Additionally, our current ministry has morphed into an archival website ministry to cover memories of those aspects, which are part of our heritage, which could have relevance today and be helpful for those wanting to change society today for the better in the future. So, this specific rendition should be supplemented and be used as a hybrid of both a written book to capture our personal reflections backed up by research documents and website material on the internet and from the Ministry pages on *https://www.candmministries.org.uk/ministry-index*. There will even be an Index of all the names of those mentioned in the printed version and their specific involvement.

We felt it was important to share much of the related history, and not only our personal memories although inevitably it is our story – as 'his-story' always is. We have made many attempts to write up the story, with different slants, approaches and with different titles, but we were also concerned that this became a comprehensive and accurate history.

A number of those rejected early efforts are available for serious researchers on request, while other chapters from different viewpoints are accessible on our website. We are also hoping to supplement the lessons learned from these years with missing aspects which had an effect on many of those involved during this period – or from those who saw the changes that took place perhaps a little differently.

Ours is inevitably a Christian perspective in an increasingly secular society where God is often being ignored or, even by some Christians, sidelined as irrelevant in the current era, but we had a vision of enabling a Christian community of believers to be proactive in initiating change in society, both church and nation. We make no apology for this.

God has good plans for those who love him – He is in control!

INTRODUCTON TO THE WHOLE STORY (not just this Volume)

The story of our ministry at Moggerhanger Park really begins in our pastoral ministry in the London area from the 1950s to the early 1990s. We had four phases of pastoral ministry beginning at Harlesden Northwest London for five years, then 10 years in Tottenham North London, followed by a further period of nearly 10 years ministry in the East End of London before moving to Lambeth in South London in the 1980s and into the 90s.

In the East End of London in the 1970s we led a community of believers with a shared faith in Jesus who were in a covenant relationship with each other, looking to God for the provision of our needs and to the Holy Spirit for the direction of our activities. It was a prayer-centred kingdom community, sharing decisions, resources and needs and was certainly positively affected by the Charismatic Renewal movement which had arisen during the postwar period of considerable change in other sectors of society. We lived and worked on the basis of kingdom principles using community development concepts, recognising each other's gifts, and seeking to develop the gifts and abilities of others in the neighbourhood as they responded to the presence and input of our little kingdom community.

It was during this long period of ministry in London that many doors were opened to national and international ministry, which brought an increasing prophetic awareness of the vast social and cultural changes that were taking place everywhere in the latter part of the 20th century. We also saw the inadequacies of the traditional churches to be proactive in communicating the word of God into a rapidly changing scene. Our wider ministry began when the Archbishop of Canterbury, Dr Donald Coggan, invited us to join him and carry out, on a national scale, what we had been doing in the East End of London. This led to our organising the 1980 'National Congress on Evangelism' and to the formation of the British Church Growth Association that Monica led for 25 years.

Not only was the BCGA formed at this time, but also Prophetic Word Ministries (known as PWM) with its links to Prayer and Parliament, as well as Prophecy Today were all launched. The Carmel/Jerusalem prophetic gatherings of 1986 took place, leading to PWM Team Ministries touring the country and setting up Issachar groups as watchmen. A cross dimensional theological educational group of thinkers and teachers, led by BCGA and PWM cooperating together, also led to the establishment of 'The Centre for Contemporary Ministry' and the formation of a ministry centre at Bawtry Hall, Yorkshire for running residential in-service training courses for clergy and church leaders. The central theme of these courses was in the first two 'Gaining a Wider Vision' and 'Turning Vision into Strategy', although many other three-to-five-day recognised and subsidised courses were developed and then opened up to lay people too. At the same time, it built up a significant resource centre as well as contributing to an international prayer movement.

As the prophetic significance of our ministry also increased, we received a promise that God would one day give us a base outside London for all these various ministries where they could be developed supporting each other. This had been first received as a promise at a team prayer meeting in the 1970s during our ministry in the East End of London, but it was not until 1991 that we were reminded of this promise. It had been recalled while seeking answers to prayer needed on a social issue for one of our prayer partners, during a team prayer meeting of the magazine Prophecy Today at our editorial office in Tower Bridge Rd, London. Cliff had a prayer picture of a building which he later recognised when we first saw Moggerhanger House. At the

London prayer time, we were given two words, presumably for its location – Bedford, and Clapham.

That time of prayer was followed a few hours later by a phone call from a minister in South Africa saying that he had just been reading one of Cliff's books and in his time of prayer he had heard God promising to give us a base for the ministry. He could not possibly have known anything about us, so it was a remarkable coincidence. We did not know the significance of the word 'Clapham' until much later after we had acquired Moggerhanger Park and discovered its links with William Wilberforce and the Clapham Sect.

It was in the late 1980s that we had begun looking for a base where we could bring together our different ministries and one of our team, Clifford Denton, who had earlier set up a trust, 'Harvest Vision', for evangelism among Muslims, suggested the basic charitable trust might be helpful as he was no longer using it. We agreed to take it and adapt it as a separate ministry to take responsibility for the acquisition and maintenance of buildings to provide a centre for all three of our then current ministries. At the same time, we were developing a prayer group in the Bedford area meeting on a weekly basis to study New Testament concepts of community beginning with the 'koinonea' of Acts 2:42.

We appointed a small group of trustees for Harvest Vision and began looking at premises in the Bedford area beginning with Clapham Park, a stately home that had been a Christian community centre run by nuns but had recently closed. The owners wanted £500,000 and, while we were attracted to it with its ready-made conference facilities including a chapel, we none of us felt quite right about it and it certainly was not the prayer picture Cliff had received. After more than two years searching for premises, we repented of all the time we had spent searching and decided to wait quietly until God revealed the place that he wanted for us to use as a Ministry Centre. That was the starting point of this book.

Chapter One
HOW IT ALL STARTED

This chapter recounts the beginning of a great venture of faith which starts with our first visit to Moggerhanger Park. This is in response to a promise from God and its fulfilment which gives us a Ministry Centre where our community of believers can be his witnesses.

In the early 1990s, we, Cliff and Monica Hill, were beginning to feel the exhilarating, but tiring, effects of travelling, nationally and internationally and leading three thriving ministries PWM, BCGA and CCM.[1]

- Prophetic Word Ministries (PWM) embraced both the printed magazine *Prophecy Today* and 'PWM Team Ministries' and was based in Tower Bridge Road, London.

- The British Church Growth Association (BCGA) were pre movers in this new mission-oriented discipline and were already coordinating a number of national and international departments and had taken a significant step of faith. In 1991, expecting to move to Clapham Park Bedford, we re-located its office headquarters and books to temporary accommodation in the centre of Bedford.

- The Centre for Contemporary Ministry (CCM) had for more than four years been running a growing number of popular in-service training courses for clergy and lay leaders as well as a national prayer and educational ministry in Bawtry Hall, near Doncaster and they had more recently been planning for a School of Ministry there.

1 History of ministries link: see *https://www.candmministries.org.uk/ministry-index*

We were living in a time of rapid social change and our ministries were seeking to influence both church and society. We realised how much more effective these national (and growing international) Ministries, could be if they were all centred in one location and working together. Then we remembered the promise God had made to us in the past that he would *'give us a Ministry Centre'*.[2]

Harvest Vision and its Trustees

We believed this centre would need to be outside London and we had recognised that owning buildings would need the involvement and coordination of many people with distinct tasks if it were to be successful. We also believed that God had told us that Bedford was where the premises would be located.

By 1988 we had already established a charity 'Harvest Vision' (HV). The Harvest Vision Trustees consisted of local Bedford-based men and women, both lay and clergy from Anglican, Baptist and Methodist local churches as well as businessmen and ministry colleagues.[3] The new trust had a number of Advisors[4] as well as Trustees and their support group was a strong and committed prayer community who were meeting regularly.

2 For more details of all the words and promises received please be in touch by e-mail: *heritage@candmministries.org.uk.*

3 This charity with its wide community support also has some background history on the website. Its 3 inaugural trustees were Peter West (Chair), Dorothy Richards (Sec), Clifford Hill (CCM & PWM) joined shortly by Monica Hill (CCM & BCGA), Andrew Ingrey-Senn (Business), Christopher Strong (Ang), Peter Dye (Bapt) and John Job (Meth).

4 Harvest Vision's advisors were Viscount Brentford, Michael Fenton Jones, Denham Gilbart Smith, Timothy Green, Christopher Hill, as well as local Bedford personalities such as Canon Malcolm Scott, Lady Howard, Lord and Lady Luke.

Harvest Vision Trustees had committed themselves to coordinate the search and carry out the technical management so that they would be ready when the right premises were found. It was their Secretary, Dorothy Richards who, in 1990 when the BCGA had suddenly lost their London offices, had provided rent-free a shopfront in central Bedford to house their headquarters, which then also became the focal point for the Harvest Vision community and the shop was renamed the 'Harvest Centre'.

Harvest Vision Community

We were coordinating a community composed of those who had the same vision and who were praying for its fulfilment, and who were also preparing themselves to play an active part. It was a large group from all over the country and also from all walks of life who by this time were planning to form a supporting residential community at Clapham Park, just outside Bedford in the centre of England where we felt the Lord was leading us.[5]

When this particular door had closed firmly, the search had continued and plans for community members selling their homes and moving on-site were put on hold.

In our search for the right premises, we had reached a point of despair. We had spent over two years in fruitless search among buildings in and around Bedford.

Instead of waiting patiently, we had spent a lot of energy running around looking for the right place – even to possibilities right outside this area and in other parts of the county. Now we were wondering if we had heard God properly. The only thing we could do was to repent and wait patiently.

---

5   The Harvest Vision praying community were the backbone of any joint action carried out and many chapters relating to its growth are now appearing on the website.

Hope Comes out of Despair

Then within one month of making that decision, Dorothy Richards, now in sole charge of the continuing search, made an unexpected phone call to us. Dorothy had many friends in Bedford where she had been in business and she phoned us at our home in East Sussex where, following a demanding period of ministry including an overseas tour, we were spending a Bank Holiday weekend in rest and prayer. She said that a local firm of developers were offering us a large old manor house. We really didn't want to see any more houses, so we wearily said, "Oh yes, how much do they want for it?" She said, "They are not asking for anything, they want to *give* it to us!" We suddenly became interested. We recalled that the wording of the promise we had received many years ago was that God would *give* us a place for the ministry, but we had never taken this literally – thinking that we had got to go out and find the place and then raise the money to purchase it.

Of course, we asked for more details. The house had been used as a school during the First World War, but since 1919 it had been adapted for use as a hospital. When a new hospital was built in Bedford the house had been sold in the 1980s to a developer. He had been unable to obtain the planning permissions required to change it into apartments or business offices due to its Grade 2 star listing. It was deteriorating badly, and the developers did not want to spend any more money on it, so they simply wanted to give it to us on condition that we would take responsibility for all essential repairs. They had obtained 'Enabling Planning Permission' for building 12 houses in the grounds to give them income for the repairs. They were only interested in the new-build houses and were willing to give us the big old house on 5 acres of ground, provided we did the repairs to it.

First Visit to Moggerhanger Park

Before alerting the other trustees, we decided to visit the premises ourselves. Early on Monday 23rd August 1993, we (Monica and Cliff) left our family home in East Sussex and drove to Moggerhanger. We climbed over a five-barred gate and fought our way through head-high grass and weeds to walk around the house and its surrounding single-storey prefabricated hospital wards. We peered in through the windows and were daunted by the sheer size of the place, as well as by the obviously poor condition of the buildings.

We, nevertheless, felt a strange witness in our spirits that this could be the place that God had promised to us. It was not easy to see the house due to several attached hospital wards, but the south elevation at the rear was exactly like Cliff had seen in a prayer picture in the PWM offices several years earlier. It was three storeys high, a flat surface with no bay windows and it was white – although rather dirty.

We were cautious but interested enough to call all our HV trustees and ask them to meet us there as soon as possible. Amazingly, they were all free to meet there on Friday that week (27th August) at 9.00am. This time we arranged the visit with the Developers, Twigden Homes, whose agent arranged for their estate manager to meet us there and show us round the premises. He took us on a conducted tour of the house and then a short way round the grounds into the areas that they as developers would retain.

Exploring the House and Estate

The interior of the house was in a terrible condition in every room. In several places plaster had been stripped from the walls and ceilings through clumsy attempts to deal with dry rot, and in the south-east corner of the drawing room there was a large gap in the ceiling, and also in the room above, so that you could see from the ground floor up to the sky through the roof. In most of the rooms there were the remnants of the hospital with bed spaces marked out for sliding curtains and hand basins for washing. Rubbish was left everywhere with coverings of dirt and dust. It was a daunting sight, but we were there to see what could be; not what existed at that moment. Monica, in particular, had been involved in bringing back into use several churches in much worse condition!

It was not possible to see the walled gardens which the Developers would be retaining, because they were entirely overgrown with weeds and head-high stinging nettles. We were, however, able to go past a fascinating Icehouse and get a little way down a path, which we at that time had called 'Broad Walk' before discovering some years later that Repton had called it 'Filbert Walk'. It ran to the south of the walled gardens and the estate manager explained that this would be where the houses were to be built and where our boundary would be. One of the houses was to breach this wall of the walled gardens and have its sun lounge built in 'Broad Walk' which would be very close to the house. Another of the new houses was to have been built right alongside the icehouse which would be part of the land being offered to us, and it too was also quite close to the front of the house.

The Promise

We both had a strong check in our spirits concerning these new houses. Although our plans were for housing and accommodation for our community, we could foresee a possible conflict of interest between the householders and ourselves, particularly when we wanted to use the house and grounds for quiet times and prayer retreats.

Cliff lagged behind the other trustees as we were walking along 'Broad Walk' around the walled gardens. He was urgently praying as he went. At that moment he received a wonderful reassurance that confirmed the rightness of our acquisition of Moggerhanger House. Quite clearly, Cliff heard God say, *'Do not worry. Those houses will never be built'*. This was a promise that was going to mean much to us in the days to come when our faith would be severely tested and when it seemed that we were the only ones prepared to fight the Developers to prevent them building much larger houses which could cause conflict with our plans for building a community.

We caught up with the party in time to hear Twigden's Estate Manager saying, quite surprisingly, that, in his opinion, these houses would never be built. He had evidently done his calculations, taking into account the considerable distance over which all the main services would have to be brought to serve just 12 houses and he had come to the conclusion that the profit margin was not sufficiently large to make the buildings viable, as presently projected.

Later, when Twigden was acquired by Kier, they were to come to the same conclusion which would result in a long and bruising battle involving the Developers, Harvest Vision, the District, and the County Council. But that comes later in the story. At that time, we immediately perceived the estate manager's words to be a prophetic statement (of the 'Balaam' type) given to confirm the words Cliff had just heard.

Those Houses Will Never Be Built

The significance for us, of that first walk around the grounds, was that from this moment we knew God was promising that the houses would never be built. We knew that his intention was to give us a home for the three Ministries in a place of peace and tranquillity protected from the world, where the most important activity would be to seek the Face of the Lord, to understand what was happening in our generation and thereby to be in a position to declare the word of God to the nation for our times from a secure base within a committed Christian community.[6]

As we finished the walk and arrived back at the house, Cliff found himself alongside one of the active Harvest Vision Trustees, Andrew Ingrey-Senn, and he said to him, "Andrew, the Lord has shown me that those houses will never be built." He acknowledged this with thankfulness. He too had heard the words of the Estate Manager and saw them as prophetic.

The importance of the promise that the houses would not be built in the grounds cannot be exaggerated. Without our belief that the promise was from God, we would not have recommended to the trustees that we should go ahead with the acquisition of Moggerhanger Park, and it is almost certain that we would have walked away from Moggerhanger. It was not our confidence in our own ability to discern the word of the Lord, but our confidence in *his concern for his Ministry* that was paramount. It is of great importance that this should be understood.

Moses' Prayer

We needed some time together to pray about our next action, so we all gathered in what had been the nurses' recreation hall in the stable courtyard, which was later to become the main Ministry Office, where we spent some time, praising God in worship, before making the momentous decision. In a time of prayer, one scripture stood out. It was the prayer of Moses

6 It was not that we did not value housing – we were of, course, looking to create a residential community at that time – but what was being planned was not the right kind of housing for our needs. It was too close and would impede our own wider vision and intentions. Even the Grading of the House as 2* did not worry us as in our limited experience this did not prevent positive use although it might be more difficult to apply for grants - but that did not phase us either as we knew that if we were doing the Lord's work, he would also supply all our needs – often through his people or in kind.

when he faced the enormous decision for leading the Israelites through the wilderness to the Promised Land. *"If your presence does not go with us, do not send us up from here"* (Ex 33:13-16). This scripture came to mean a great deal to us. We all knew that unless God was in this venture, we were heading for disaster.

Shared Decisions

Later that day our son, Stephen, and our daughter Jenny and her husband Simon, who were later to play an important part in the life of Moggerhanger Park, joined us there to look at the house and the estate. We all agreed that despite its dilapidated appearance, the vast amount of work needed, and the terrible state of the grounds, it would make an excellent Ministry Centre. The next stage was to bring our small 'community of believers' to see the house and either endorse or veto the decision of the Harvest Vision trustees who would not have gone ahead without the full backing of this community.

They also confirmed that this was the right place. We communicated the news to the three sets of Ministry Trustees and then the whole PWM team from London went to Ashburnham Place, Sussex for a planned three-day retreat appropriately enough on the theme of Exodus 33:12-16.

During the following month there were numerous meetings with planning officers, surveyors, architects, and business advisers, but everything pointed to the rightness of going ahead with the decision to proceed with negotiations with the Developers. Twigden wanted us to enter a legal contract that we would carry out the repairs agreed with Mid-Beds D.C. at an estimated cost of £350,000, within a year of our signing the contract.

Lack of Money

A major difficulty was that we did not have the money in hand to back up our claim that we could carry out the necessary repairs.[7] We assured Twigden that we were a Christian Ministry with a sound record and a strong support base. We told them that we were a faith ministry, only concerned with prophets (spelt differently!) and not used to building up a financial profit and that God always supplied what was needed for our work and he would supply the £350,000 that was needed at the right time.

The developers, however, preferred a letter from the bank manager saying that we had £350,000 already in our account. This was not possible since our total known assets from all three ministries were only about £50,000!

At the beginning of November, Andrew Ingrey-Senn had a meeting with Twigden's Managing Director where a time limit was imposed by the developers that we had to have the full amount of money in hand by the end of the month. They said there was someone else interested in the property and they would not be patient with us for much longer. Then on 11th November they rang Andrew to say that their Board had decided to drop Harvest Vision and to accept the offer of another developer.

This was a real test of faith for all the Trustees. For us personally it was pivotal, because we were so sure that God had led us to Moggerhanger and that this was the place he intended for our ministry base.

Doubts

Of course, doubts creep in at times like this. Cliff had to face the question, 'Did I really hear the voice of the Lord speaking to me, or was it my imagination?'

---

7   We had accepted that this was the sum needed for essential repairs for the roof and areas where we could not carry out the repairs ourselves – and that these would enable the Developers to make the gift of the House to us - but we intended moving forward by becoming much more 'hands on' and involved with our wide prayer partner base to carry out the work ourselves.

The following 24 hours were extremely demanding. Monica was finalising an issue of the Church Growth Digest for the printer,[8] Cliff had to write the editorial for *Prophecy Today*, prepare to speak at a large public meeting in the City Temple in London the next day (Saturday 13th November) and we were both preparing to lead and speak at a three-day conference in Swanwick, Derbyshire.

We both often work better under pressure and Cliff sometimes finds it easier to hear from the Lord in urgent times rather than when he is at leisure. Monica often does not sleep well anyway (and she writes her best articles in the night hours) and Cliff often cuts down his sleep to 4 or 5 hours a night in order to cope with the volume of work and still have sufficient time to get before the Lord to hear what he is saying. There was a real sense of urgency now in seeking to know what God was saying to us in these desperate times, when it appeared that we had already lost everything.

Decision-Time

Strangely enough, in spite of all the pressure, we both had a tremendous sense of peace, as though we were being shown that this was simply a proving-ground for the testing days that lay ahead. Quite clearly, the Lord had said to us that Moggerhanger was the place of his choice.

We were both convinced that he was now saying, "*Do not be afraid, for this is the place that I have given you.*" We then received specific instructions what to do. We telephoned Peter West, our HV chairman, and Andrew Ingrey-Senn and told them that God had confirmed that he had given Moggerhanger Park to us and that within three days Twigden would come back to us asking to re-commence negotiations. It was, therefore,

8 Her team was scattered around the country and at that time magazines needed to be edited, typeset and collated by hand before going to be printed.

essential that we were in a position to give them the guarantees that they required.

A Crucial Letter

Cliff and Monica then sat down to finalise the draft letter to go out to all the Prayer Partners and supporters in the PWM Ministry, members of the British Church Growth Association and those on the mailing list of the Centre for Contemporary Ministry, as well as all the Harvest Vision community. The letter stated that God had led us to Moggerhanger Park, in fulfilment of his promise to give us a Ministry Centre, but we had to demonstrate our ability to carry out the essential repairs in order to satisfy the developers. We let them know that we had therefore opened a Harvest Vision bank account in Bedford, just a few doors from Monica's shop front offices.

We gave the number of the account saying we believed that by the end of November (1993) there would be £350,000 in that account so that we could complete the negotiations. We said that we had told the developers that our God would supply, and we were certain that he would keep his promise. We asked them to pray and that if they felt able to help, either by a gift or through making an interest-free loan, we would be very grateful.

After the meeting at the City Temple in London, attended by some 2000 people, we went to the PWM office in Tower Bridge Road with Jean Wolton, our secretary, to finalise the letter to all these Prayer Partners and then we drove home to East Sussex for a day of prayer and preparation. That same Sunday evening, we took the copy of the letter and delivered it to our friendly prayer partner printers in Folkestone, having promised our trustees that we would not post the letter until Twigden did come back to us. We were quite certain that they would do so.

With this confidence we gave the letter so that it could be printed on Monday 15th November. The following day, Tuesday

16th, two of our supporters in Folkestone, Margaret and Malcolm Baker, spent the day folding them and putting them into envelopes, some 3,000 copies, so that they would be ready for posting. We had given strict instructions that they were to be ready for the post; but none were to be mailed until we gave the word. That same day we set off for Swanwick, Derbyshire, to lead the conference.

The Developers Return

At one o'clock the following day, Wednesday 17th November, Andrew Ingrey-Senn called on Cliff's mobile at the conference to say that Twigden's Directors had just called him to say that when they had met with the other developer the previous day, they did not believe they were 'dealing with men of integrity'. They said that they believed that we were trustworthy and so they had come back to us and wanted to resume negotiations towards the signing of a contract – the three-day promise was fulfilled.

Andrew and Cliff prayed together over the phone giving much praise and thanksgiving to God who is faithful to keep his promises. For us it was a wonderful confirmation that we were rightly hearing from the Lord. We immediately got back on the phone in the middle of the conference at Swanwick and gave the instruction to post the letters. It was an historic moment!

The following day, while we were still at Swanwick, Jean from the London office rang, to say that the phone had hardly stopped ringing with people who wanted to help, and that one man had already promised an interest-free loan of £100,000. We shared this with the people at the conference and there was great rejoicing and much praising of the Lord.

The First Moggerhanger Miracle

Even more joy was to follow. By the end of the month (the deadline set for us to respond to Twigden with confirmation that we had the money in hand for the essential repairs), when we examined our bank account there was not just £350,000, but £500,000!! We were simply overwhelmed with the goodness of the Lord and his faithfulness in giving us more than we asked. God obviously knew our needs before we knew them.

The first of the donors had been Crispin and Gill Joynson-Hicks (Viscount and Lady Brentford): Crispin was one of our original prayer partners and the lawyer who had set up our original 'C and M Ministries' charity following the 1980 National Congress on Evangelism when we first went independent, and he and his firm had since then given guidance on setting up BCGA and actually set up PWM and other charities. They had also warned us, from a personal standpoint, to be careful in taking on a listed building, as there could be many problems! Nevertheless, they gave their support – and our friendship continued.

Our negotiators went back to Twigden to reopen negotiations. At the gateway, just inside the entrance to the estate, there were two semi-detached houses and some 200 yards farther into the estate there was a bungalow. Twigden were intending selling these off separately, but we said we would like them to be included in the deal. Both the bungalow and the houses had been built in the hospital years and rendered uninhabitable and boarded up with most of their windows broken, bathrooms smashed and ceilings torn down. The developers blamed 'vandalism' but we suspected that it had been done deliberately to avoid paying council tax.

Twigden agreed to sell them to us for £130,000 (the going rate), plus a further £20,000 for the stable courtyard buildings which they said were also not included in the deal on the Main House. In fact, they threatened to sell off each of these separately. Together they came to the sum of £150,000 which, with the £350,000 for the repairs, came to £500,000 – exactly the figure that we had in the bank! God's wisdom in providing for our needs is far greater than ours![9]

We saw this as tremendous confirmation of the rightness of going ahead with the acquisition of Moggerhanger House and estate. We also saw it as a tremendous sign of the faithfulness of God. For us, personally, it was a joy to know that we had rightly heard from the Lord and that the steps of faith we had urged the trustees to take had not been foolhardy or reckless but had been based upon a true word from God.

The House and Park for £1

Twigden's board met on 7th December 1993 and formally agreed to sell Moggerhanger House plus 15 acres of parkland to Harvest Vision for £1 (the trustees fell over each other to give the £1 – so the Lord's promise to *give* us premises was literally fulfilled!) and the £350,000 was set aside in a dedicated fund at the bank for the restoration. Twigden additionally agreed to sell the remaining buildings on the estate comprising the two gatehouses, the bungalow, and the stable courtyard buildings for the sum of £150,000.

This was the first of the Moggerhanger miracles and we could do no other than praise God for his goodness in the words of Psalm 66: *"Shout with joy to God, all the earth! Sing the glory of his name, make his praise glorious! Say to God, 'How awesome are your deeds!'"*

9 Many of these donations were anonymous and later when it came to the annual audit, our meticulous auditor queried the fact that there was more money in the account than receipts held by the bank – but we let them sort this out!

Chapter Two
OCCUPYING THE ESTATE

We learn some important lessons about listening to God and moving in his timing. We begin our occupation of Moggerhanger Park and welcome many of our prayer partners to Open Days. Then we hold our first series of Bible teaching meetings.

Planning the Future

Having seen what we believed to be the Lord's provision for the acquisition of Moggerhanger Park, we were full of hope and eagerness to get going. Mark Eddison, who was a member of our former church at St Marks, Kennington, London, had been advising us architecturally and understood the kind of community accommodation we needed, and he agreed to start drawing up plans. Having requested donations to be paid directly into their new bank account, Dorothy, on behalf of Harvest Vision, had found it rather difficult to identify and thank all those who had sent in their gifts, as well as manage a new mailing list, so our little shop front in Bedford and the volunteers who were keen to work on the project even in this early stage became very active and fulfilled.

Although our offer had been accepted, we had not realised that the legal transfer would take as long as it did, and that prior to that, we would have to request permission to visit or start any necessary work. We did, though, want to have an Open Day for our Prayer Partners to rejoice with us as soon as possible so that we could also begin to think through, and share with them, all that had to be done.

We recognised that for a period Harvest Vision and BCGA would be the prime movers as they were the nearest of the

Partnership Groups as both were based at that time in Bedford, and the Harvest Vision community could be mobilised more easily, to take any necessary practical action.

CCM was already operating at Bawtry Hall, on a similar model to other trusts in the Hall. Action Partners,[1] the owners and key players, were keen to help us, but we could not just up-root CCM's courses and bring everything down to Moggerhanger – their offices and the bedrooms for their main residential courses needed to be prepared and in place, and PWM, with its magazine *Prophecy Today* was in a distribution cycle and plans for moving essential staff from the London office needed to be planned very carefully.

Dreaming Dreams

We were able to examine our architect, Mark Eddison's, plans, in order to prioritise action and move towards the buildings being able to serve our long-term vision. The ministry administration needed to come first: this was to be located in the Stable Courtyard area, which we imagined might be easier – alongside which we needed to bring back into use the Gatehouses and Bungalow to accommodate volunteers – as currently this was a faith project and we had as yet no additional funding for anything.

Facing Reality

Twigden had insisted that the full estimated cost of £350,000 to cover essential repairs which we had raised, was deposited in a special account and used to settle accounts with contractors who needed to be appointed, and so was no longer available to us to draw upon.

So, we also established a dedicated Volunteers Expenses Fund through which we could provide cover for activities and

1   Action Partners (charity 225364) was the UK residential training base for the Sudan United Mission which gave us international and prayer links and figures more in the story.

some food and travel support for long-term residents. Most of those who came, were able not only to give their time but also to provide for their own travel and food, often bringing with them tools to carry out the work as well as gifts for others, but we did not want to exclude those who could only give their time. The Fund was managed carefully – but there always seemed to be sufficient.

Future Potential

We could see that the Main House would be the central activity base. Its main use would be as an education centre starting with residential clergy in-service training courses which CCM were currently running at the rate of two each month at Bawtry Hall Yorkshire. Lyn Wortley had been our excellent Administrator locally from the beginning, soon to be joined by Meg Booth who oversaw the books and resources for the courses. The courses had gained accreditation by Church Denominations and the demand was there for more courses to give a wider range, and to provide sabbaticals and consultations for church leaders. Russ and Lesley Howell carried out the Chaplaincy role on the courses and all follow up. The In-Service Courses were supplemented by BCGA and PWM with lecturers already running their courses in different parts of the country. The potential for widening this use was there through our Parliamentary ministry where Christian MPs could come to seek the Lord together.

The European Church Growth Association also was already active and links were developing even wider afield bringing diverse groups together. Currently our own speakers and teams were travelling on national tours, using churches who were keen to make their premises available for local and regional events for both BCGA and PWM but we had a vision for Moggerhanger Park being able to provide the base for people to come to us rather than us needing to travel to them.

Additionally, the resources we were producing, which were being shared and circulated with those who came regularly to meet the team, were endless. Church Growth was in a new stage as a distinctive work, with a Church Growth Book Service operating from a Scottish base as well as a growing Church Growth Lending Library. This was already expanding with materials and resources essential for the educational courses being run by CCM.

A 'World Mission Study Centre' was an important project planned by CCM and increasingly was being emphasised by the other two ministries: PWM had already developed a Biblical and Hebraic Roots Study Centre, following the 1986 Carmel / Jerusalem conference. The aim of the Centre was to examine the Hebraic roots of the Christian faith, and to explore in depth the insights that could be offered to many people in the churches. These were all expected to be distinctive features for which Moggerhanger Park would become known.

Operating Plans

It had also been our intention to have the Harvest Vision Community as a resident community living in their own homes on or near the estate. Any thoughts we might have had of encouraging members of the Community to buy new homes from Twigden were dashed when we heard God say, '*these houses will never be built*'. We had to put these plans on hold and find other ways of building up the 'community of believers'.

Although the two Gatehouses and Bungalow were a tremendous resource as community property, as they could provide fully-furnished, self-serviced space for those involved on the estate or in the offices short or long-term, we were encouraging anyone occupying these to have their own property that they could return to at any time. We encouraged those who could, of the wider community, to move their homes into the village and live locally, but we could also see the potential of extending the Gatehouses to service the estate in this way providing for a continuing base for the community.

Booking the Grand Opening

It had been our original intention to get at least PWM and BCGA on-site and to have carried out the clearing and those essential repairs on the house which were beyond our means as quickly as possible and then begin appealing to our many supporters throughout the country to come armed with their toolboxes and paint brushes to help us transform the inside of the house with volunteer labour. We expected to have 'work parties' throughout the summer of 1994, and that the house would be fully operational by the spring of 1995.

In this confidence we booked the date for the Grand Opening of Moggerhanger House on Saturday 29th April 1995. We booked Viscountess Gill Brentford and the Right Revd John Taylor, Bishop of St Albans, to perform the opening ceremony.

Getting it Wrong!

In the event, we got the timing spectacularly wrong! Far from having the Grand Opening in the spring of 1995, by that date we had only just completed the purchase of the estate! It was the beginning of learning lessons of the folly of running ahead driven by enthusiasm rather than being led by dependence upon God.

We certainly learned the necessity of seeking guidance step by step. In addition, we knew that our lives were becoming even more greatly overloaded. We were commuting regularly between our home near Rye in East Sussex, our separate ministry offices in central London and Bedford, and our teaching base in Bawtry Hall in Yorkshire.

2 Occupying the Estate

We both spoke at many meetings with our respective teams in different parts of Britain and at that time PWM especially was dealing with the fallout from the 'Toronto Blessing' that was affecting churches all over Britain. We had expected to organise a church leaders' consultation at Moggerhanger, but it was held instead in Bawtry Hall in February 1995. All three of our Ministries were involved which led to the publication of the book *Blessing the Church?* which examines the roots of the 'Blessing', still used as a reference book today.

Alongside being Editor-in-Chief of *Prophecy Today* as well as being PWM's prime mover, somehow Cliff also managed to keep up his writing, publishing not only *Blessing the Church?*[2] during that year but also a revised version of *Prophecy Past and Present* which won a prize in the USA as theological 'Book of the Year 1991', and a booklet *Charismatic Crossroads*, all very topical issues at the time. This was all before the PWM office moved its base to Moggerhanger in September 1995.

Monica also was running on overload as she was a Trustee of PWM and involved in most of its meetings around the country with Cliff, as well as writing a regular page for *Prophecy Today* on 'World Mission'. This was all in addition to her being the Executive Director of the British Church Growth Association, editor of the *Church Growth Digest* and overseeing the BCGA office in Bedford. Additionally, during this period, she was the first President of the European Church Growth Association which involved her in a lot of cross-Channel travel. And as if that was not enough, she now also oversaw the volunteers and work on the Moggerhanger estate.

2 'Blessing the Church?' was a symposium from papers given at a conference held at Bawtry Hall in 1995

Working on Overload

It was some time before we faced the fact that we were not spending enough time seeking the Lord concerning the house – we were sitting back and letting everything just drift on and it needed us to be even more active! Of course, we had our quiet times for writing and preparation for speaking engagements, but we could not give all the time that was necessary to the needs of Moggerhanger House. We were carried by the euphoria of knowing that we had made the right decision, and we took it for granted that everything would flow smoothly from that moment.

On the contrary, the problems and challenges seemed to come thick and fast, not least of which was the intransigence of Twigden's solicitors on completing the transfer of Moggerhanger Park to Harvest Vision – they sometimes took months to respond to questions from our solicitors. We later discovered that they were going slow because Twigden were exploring ways of selling their business.

Monica's Act of Faith and the First Ministry Occupation

Looking back, it was in September 1994, immediately after our second Open Day for our Prayer Partners but a full six-months before we had any legal ownership of the estate, that Monica took yet another step of faith with the consent of her BCGA Council (trustees) from all over the country, who obviously trusted her judgement! It helped a little on unifying activities as she moved the BCGA central office from Bedford into a small room on the ground floor in the centre of the stable courtyard buildings designated as offices so that her travel commitments were reduced, and she could be on-site to cover any eventuality. The first Ministry, with its coordinating skills, had arrived at Moggerhanger Park.

The volunteers had by this time, taken steps to make the central space in the western Courtyard buildings habitable by reroofing it. We later discovered this area had been the manure heap of the stables. We were already in the business of transformation!

This room served as Harvest Vision's office and as our Ministry Centre, until we had full ownership of the estate. The large number of specialist Church Growth books were all stored in a cleared space in a corner of the newly named Garden Room[3] while plans were drawn up for developing this into a library. The shop front in Bedford had served us well for three years but we were pleased to be entering a new era with even greater potential.

Work on the Bungalow, as well as the Gatehouses, from then onwards carried on alongside that on the wider estate and in clearing the Main House. Dorothy's flat and home in Biddenham was still serving us well, both for meetings and our personal use, but we felt that we could be more effective if we were resident permanently on-site as soon as possible. Not wanting to use much needed funds and resources which were being provided for the ministry on making the Bungalow habitable for us to occupy, hopefully long-term, we set about leasing out our family home near Rye. This would provide us with the necessary funds to repair the Bungalow although it was August 1996 before we moved our furniture in and took up full residence.

First Open Days

The community of believers played an enormous part in the foundation of the whole Moggerhanger Park project. They were

---

3   We were negotiating to keep Ward 6 from the hospital days to use for community work while the Main House was being made useable. Thia became the Garden Room – more about the demolition of the other wards in the next chapter.

not only steadfast in prayer, but they were eager to give practical help. During the year of legal negotiations, Twigden gave us permission to hold a community day on the estate, using the stable courtyard buildings on the May Bank Holiday Monday in 1994. This gave an opportunity for supporters to meet the community who had been meeting for prayer and fellowship for over four years enjoying more recently the security of the 'Harvest Centre' in nearby Bedford, to focus on Moggerhanger as a specific site in the future.

In preparation for this first historic community event, we organised a workday on Saturday 30th April 1994. About 50 people arrived from all parts of the country and carried out many tasks – clearing paths, cutting down weeds, locating water supplies and electricity services, cleaning rooms, and generally preparing for the expected visit of many supporters.

One of our memories was of buying two lengths of hosepipe (each 100 metres long) as the only mains water we could find was in a tap in the walled gardens from which we ran a pipe to the toilets and kitchen in the old stables. We also recall using 'walkie talkies' to communicate as there were no telephone fittings available, mobile phones were limited and bulky, and the area we were working on was vast! Still another, caught on video, is the basic guidance we gave to those willing to take visitors around the inside of the house – our first Tour Guides!

About 300 people came on Bank Holiday Monday 2nd May 1994 and we had a great time of prayer and praise, with tours of the house and grounds in the morning, culminating in the blowing of a shofar to co-ordinate a call to prayer. This was necessary as we could not easily encircle the house due to all the prefabricated hospital wards stretching out into the grounds, so groups gathered at various points around the house. They brought their own seating and refreshments, and the afternoon was given to praise and worship on the grass at the back of the house led by Andrew and the music team from Bromham Baptist Church.

A second Open Day on Saturday 23rd July brought even larger numbers of our prayer partners from afar, and a third one was planned for September 1994 – these were the start of opening the house and grounds to others, each demonstrating the growing level of support among our prayer partners,

Establishing a Residential Workforce

From the July 1994 'Open Day', the developers had allowed us to have one or two of our community permanently on-site – ostensibly to take responsibility for the security of the house which we did from that time onward. This was the beginning of the ministry of Harvest Vision at Moggerhanger Park. During the two days of preparation in July 1994, Mike Baker had brought his tent, and he became our first resident. One or two others who had a distance to travel had done likewise including Dave Hellens from Folkestone, and still others stayed with local members of the community making it a long weekend.

Mike was soon joined by Brian Privett, who became our resident plumber and he found somewhere to sleep in an upstairs room in the stable courtyard area. Brian and Mike stayed on-site on a semi-permanent basis, and they were soon joined by David Fawkes from Lincolnshire who had electrical skills. These three not only looked after the security of the estate and the house, but also did numerous jobs of a practical nature and formed a small resident community base and reference point for others coming on-site to help. They each gave invaluable voluntary service in preparing the buildings, including the Bungalow and Gatehouses, for future occupation. There was a limit though, in what we could do because we still did not own the estate!

Hospital Wards Demolished

Early in September 1994, before we held our third Open Day, Twigden had carried out their contractual obligation (agreed with the Mid-Beds Council) to demolish the old, prefabricated hospital wards that surrounded the house. By arrangement with Harvest Vision, they left the most westerly one nearest to the planned offices that we were already finding invaluable, and this ward became our major community meeting area for many years and was renamed 'The Garden Room'.

Prior to the complete destruction and removal of some 7 or 8 wards around the House, our three resident volunteers, plus numerous visiting volunteers, spent a great deal of time and energy in stripping them of anything that might be useful to us in the future. Many of the ward floors had been made of wood parquet blocks which were carefully removed and stacked as being of potential value, as were many of the electrical fittings which David thought could be reused as needed. They even set aside a hydro-therapy pool with its surrounding walls which we thought could be used for a baptismal pool – we were dreaming dreams! We still expected to do most of the repair work on the house ourselves using our prayer partners,

The demolition of the wards left the house exposed for the first time in 70 years so that, by the Open Day on 17th September 1994, the whole of the original house could be seen. This enabled us to form a prayer chain physically right around the house for the first time and then to go inside, room by room praying and dedicating the place for its future service. Progress was being made at last!

Exchange and Completion

Legally though, we were still only on the estate on a 'grace and favour' basis, and it was not until 5th January 1995 that contracts were exchanged with completion on 8th March 1995. The legal delays inevitably set back the whole programme of work on the house. It had been made clear to us that any work on the premises would have to be undone if the sale fell through!

We were so confident that this was the place that God had given to us that we had gone ahead with work in the Stable Courtyard buildings, with our resident volunteers. This had included restoring and setting aside a small room for Harvest Vision and Monica's use – our first office at Moggerhanger. Up until she moved the BCGA headquarters there, as already reported, she had been overseeing and coordinating the work of volunteers whenever she came up to visit Dorothy and their then base in Mill Street in Bedford. She and Cliff would also come for Harvest Vision meetings, when they both stayed with Dorothy Richards in a self-contained flat at her home in Biddenham.

Change of Developers

In the spring of 1995, after we had at last completed negotiations with Twigden for the transfer of the House, we discovered they had been bought out by Kier. This was a disappointment because we had also been negotiating with Twigden to buy from them the walled gardens and woodland area, knowing they had doubts about the viability of building the 12 small houses. They had mentioned the sum of three-quarters of a million pounds as the minimum price for the land, but they offered to delay our payment of this until the restoration of the house was completed. Kier, the new owners, were not interested in selling. We were bitterly disappointed, but later we were able to look back and thank God that he did not allow us to become burdened with such a huge debt that was not specifically for ministry that could have taken us years to clear. Clearly, God had other plans in not giving us the land at this time.

But we knew that we should not worry over much as by retaining the Garden Room, we could keep up the momentum of activities on-site and involving people in creating community space.

Early Community Meetings

As the Garden Room was being developed with its own facilities including a refreshment point, we began to make arrangements for Bantree Buildings, a local firm, to erect an attached purpose-built prefabricated toilet section. We also have many memories of help coming unexpectedly – an important confirmation was from David Logan, living in Luton and the Chief Engineer for the County Council, but also a prayer partner. On a personal visit and not dressed for the occasion, he personally explored the drainage and sewer system installed by the Hospital in that part of the grounds which he felt were rather unique - and he thanked us for permission as he did not get many opportunities for practical involvement in his governmental role!

Early on, we invited all the ministers and clergy from local churches in Bedford and the surrounding areas to view the premises and discuss ways in which they might use the resources to support their work. Local youth leaders were similarly invited. These meetings helped the ministry to establish valuable links with local churches and to dispel fears in the village that we were some strange sect.

The main problem for meetings was always a lack of chairs! When the first prayer days were held in the grounds, people were asked to bring their own garden chairs to sit on. By early 1995, a few odd pieces of furniture had been donated, but people often had to perch on tables or even sit on the floor! We managed as the weather was good and we could be outdoors, but we knew this was going to be a potential problem.

Most of the buildings on the estate were derelict, but thanks to the hard work of many volunteers, the stables were the first to be made habitable as they had been earmarked as office accommodation for the ministries. The larger room, which had been the nurses' Sports Hall was used for meetings before it became the main ministry office.

We knew we were going to need Mark's architectural help on restructuring all the buildings for our use and ensuring that we completed the essential repairs on the house to the satisfaction of Twigden Homes – now Kier – and Mark[4] officially took on this responsibility as our architect and produced the first full plans in 1994 not just of the Stables area but of the Main House and other areas including the Gatehouses – we personally used another architect for making the Bungalow habitable.

PWM, who were converting the former Sports Hall into offices were funding this from their PWM supporters. Work on the Main House started with repairing the roof which was necessary before other essential repairs could be carried out.

Exploring Roots

While all this practical work was going on to provide a base on which we could build, we had been intrigued by the Grade 2 nature of the building and wanted to know more about who had lived there and how it had gained this status. We knew a little of its more recent history when it had been used as a school and a hospital before we took over, but going further back, we wanted to know more about the owners who had commissioned an architect for the original Main House, and who had designed the grounds.

The name John Soane came up in conversation and we knew there was a Soane Museum in London not too far from our present offices, so we booked an appointment and in February 1995 we made our first of what was to become many visits. We met with Helen Dorey, a fellow Christian who was an assistant curator there, who was excited to hear of our purchase.

When we were asked to put on gloves to look at the original plans for Moggerhanger House, we knew that there was bound to be some historic significance. Helen spoke about Peter Inskip, who was an authority on Soane's architectural works. He was a

4   Mark had been one of our church members at St Mark's Kennington.

close neighbour and had been following the progress of the sale, so we got in touch with him and invited him to tell us more of its history.

Although Peter had no Christian background and did not show much interest in what we were doing with the building today, he agreed to come on Saturday 29th May 1995 as part of our ministry open Bank Holiday weekend and repeat a lecture which he had given at London University earlier in the year with slides showing the original drawings and plans drawn up for the house by Sir John Soane. He also gave us a conducted tour of the house when he told us about the original usage of the building we had just bought and then asked our permission for access to carry out more research.[5] We remember Peter insisting that we were holding something precious for posterity and telling us that the building would still be there for the next group of occupants when our time as Christians was over!! Little did we know at that time how much this would affect our use in the future! We went forward in faith, feeling confident that this was the Lord's will, and that the history of the house could be included in our vision for its use.

First Lectures and Teaching Days in the Garden Room

By arrangement with the Mid-Beds planners, we had been able to retain just that one ward, 'The Garden Room', which proved such a blessing in those early days. This had given us a hall potentially seating up to 200 people although, of course, as we mentioned earlier, we did not, as yet, have any seating! We celebrated our ownership commencing in the spring of 1995 by starting a series of Saturday teaching days on the message of the biblical prophets and their relevance for today, filling

---

5 He has a great interest in the Eating Room with its great pillars.

the Garden Room with people bringing their own seating and borrowing other chairs from friendly churches.

Two of the older members of the HV community, Bert and Mary Godfrey, who were stalwart Methodists in the neighbouring village Willington, came to the rescue, and from that time, whenever chairs were needed, they personally brought over the folding chairs from their church and undertook to take them back so that they were available for Sunday services there. This commitment was evident in so many ways in others too.

We had chosen a fitting theme for the beginning of ministry at Moggerhanger Park, which symbolised our commitment to Hebraic teaching combined with the major objective of the ministries to apply biblical principles to the great social and spiritual issues of the day. Cliff did the first public lecture on the message of the Prophet Jeremiah on Saturday 4th March 1995 – four days *before* our official ownership of the property! The following week there was a further lecture on Jeremiah given by Dr John Job, chairman of the Centre for Contemporary Ministry (CCM). Others followed on Isaiah, Malachi and Amos given by Walter Riggans, Edmund Heddle, and David Noakes.

Hebraic Roots of the Faith

On each Saturday during the month of June 1995 there were further teaching days from 10am until 4pm on the theme, '*The Hebraic Roots of the Faith*'. Speakers on these days were David Pileggi and David Dolan (both from Israel), John Fieldsend and David Forbes. The well attended meetings laid the foundation for the future of the Biblical and Hebraic Centre founded by David Forbes. This was to become an important part of PWM's ministry which would be continued by CCM and later by Issachar Ministries. A further series of teaching days was held in the autumn of 1995 on the New Testament teaching on '*The*

Ministry and Gifts of the Holy Spirit' led by Monica and other leaders from the BCGA .

Immediate Answers to Prayer

The New Year of 1995 had also seen the beginning of Wednesday prayer meetings, the first being on 25th January. On that same day a number of volunteers, using various means of transport, drove to St Albans where Verulam House, a training centre owned by the Diocese, was closing. They had offered to give us any furniture, or books from the house that would be useful for Moggerhanger. We spent the evening and the following two days there, moving quantities of beds, bedding, a few more chairs, kitchen furniture, chapel furniture – including a communion table and lectern – as well as a large number of books from their library accompanied by shelving.

Growth of Meetings for Prayer

The monthly prayer mornings were attended by ministry staff and volunteers as well as by regular supporters. The meetings were led by members of the ministry team, with times of worship and teaching, and an update on the work at The Park which led into intercessory prayer for any specific concerns. Daily prayers were held in the Garden Room led by Gillian Orpin, who later was ordained in Scotland, and on her return 5 years later was appointed Chaplain.

Resident Ministries Begin

Throughout our first year of ownership, until September 1995 when the main offices had been completed and PWM had moved their offices from London to Moggerhanger (leaving CCM still active in Bawtry Hall – they did not move until 1997), the BCGA was the only resident Ministry. They not only provided office facilities for Harvest Vision but also dealt with numerous queries, visitors, builders, and surveyors, as well as visits from the local authority and the merely curious who wanted to see what was happening at what had previously been Park Hospital.

The volunteers became the public face of the community of believers at Moggerhanger Park. Many of them had been part of the small group who had laid the prayer foundations for the whole enterprise. Without their help and practical contribution, at a time when money was scarce, it would not have been possible to get the work started. They were not only a group of willing workers, but they formed a praying community with a shared vision, bringing everything before the Lord in prayer and then having the determination as well as the skills to put plans into action.

Bungalow Garden Party

As already noted, the planned opening of Moggerhanger Park as a Ministry Centre had been booked since early 1994 to take place on Saturday 29th April 1995. and Gill Brentford and John Taylor, had both agreed to take part in the opening celebrations. However by the New Year of 1995, when we had not even obtained legal ownership of the estate and the work of restoration of the main house had not yet begun, the 'Grand Opening' was deferred indefinitely.

Instead, on that chosen and well publicised day 29th April 1995 we held an 'At Home' in the large front garden of the partially renovated Bungalow at The Park. Many of our supporters, who had had that date booked for some time, came and joined with us in celebrating the goodness of God in what had been achieved so far, despite all the delays and difficulties that had been encountered. In preparation for this, a considerable amount of work had been done on the Bungalow, although it would not be ready to move into for a few more months.

Chapter Three
MINISTRY BEGINS

Negotiations with the Developers are eventually concluded. We make progress in exploring the heritage of Moggerhanger House. Priority is given to preparing PWM's self-financed office and they move in. English Heritage get involved and give the first major secular grant. Restoration work on the house begins and there is a dangerous accident, but no one is hurt.

The Spiritual Battle Begins

Prayer was a very important part of life at Moggerhanger from the beginning and as we have reported, from the New Year 1995 regular prayer days were held at The Park on the first Wednesday of each month. The first full day of prayer had been held on 9th November 1994, before we owned the estate, for the specific purpose of praying to break the deadlock in the protracted legal negotiations so that we could agree the contract for the acquisition of the house and estate and move into action.

During the 15 months of negotiations, it became increasingly clear that this was not just a legal battle on the technicalities of transferring ownership from the developers to HV, but it was a major spiritual battle that had to be fought in prayer.

At that time neither the developers nor their solicitors had any great confidence in the ability of Harvest Vision to carry out the restoration of the house which was the prerequisite for their building of the new houses in the grounds – their sole continuing interest in the estate. They were not used to doing business with charities – their values were commercial and so different – and they had no real concept of 'public benefit'. They regarded us as a bunch of Christians with good ideals but lacking in professional ability, even though our Trustees had been chosen for having recognised qualified secular skills. The developers examined in minute detail every possible contingency in tying Harvest Vision down 'through the imposition of contractual obligations' to ensure that they were able to obtain their commercial objectives.

One of the sticking points was the shared driveway and their insistence upon retaining ownership of this so that they could pass on rights of entry to the purchasers of their houses. Harvest Vision were only to be given certain rights of access, but we could already foresee serious problems for the future if the houses were built.

Legal Problems

When we had raised the original £350,000 to cover essential repairs, Twigden had insisted that it was deposited in a special bank account from which cheques could only be drawn on the signature of HV's solicitor and the developers' Managing Director. These were then payable to the contractor on production of an architect's certificate as each part of the agreed work was completed.

The concern of the Developers in creating this original restricted section of the account, from their point of view, was to ensure that all the pre-conditions covering the essential repairs on the house were completed so that the Mid-Beds planners would give permission for the new houses they were building to be occupied. Although Twigden actually had permission to build the houses, they could not be occupied until the essential repairs on the House had been completed, so Keir did not risk starting building until they were quite sure that we had repaired the roof and we could fulfil our legally contracted obligations.

Relationships with Twigden Homes had never been easy, but the new owners Keir proved to be even more difficult. Their solicitors ensured that their interests were safeguarded with long gaps between each round of correspondence. Kier were also no longer interested in building the small dwellings for which planning permission had been given. Their only interest was in maximising the profit on the land, by building large superior houses – which some of their own Directors wanted to occupy!!

All these problems and delays increasingly highlighted for us the importance of prayer. The whole purpose of Moggerhanger Park as a Ministry Centre and a place of quiet for prayer meant our teaching and community-based activities depended upon the surroundings of the house being free from the commercial enterprise that was the objective of the developers. Our objectives were in diametric opposition to theirs.

If they achieved their purpose of building large houses with superb facilities to attract wealthy homeowners, we could foresee endless disputes that would make the use of Moggerhanger Park impossible as a place of prayer and worship. We knew that only God's intervention could prevent the developers from achieving their purpose. We did not know how God would accomplish this, but we knew the importance of prayer for preparing the way for the Lord to bring to fulfilment the vision he had given to us.

Work and Prayer

Combined 'Work and Prayer Days' became major features of the activities at Moggerhanger right from the time of the first Open Day in May 1994. Saturday workdays attracted many volunteers who brought their tents and caravans to enjoy camping weekends, helping with clearing the grounds and making the Stable Courtyard buildings, Garden Room, Bungalow, and Gatehouses – all the ancillary buildings –habitable. The community of believers was growing in number and significance and we were laying the foundations of the whole enterprise.

By the time legal contracts were signed and payment made on 8th March 1995, more than a hundred volunteers (many professionals in their specific fields) had been taking an active part in this work. More importantly, the community of believers who founded the work at Moggerhanger Park had not only grown numerically, but also in their faith and their commitment to the vision of living and working as a community with a special mission, an *ekklesia* – a group with a purpose. They were preparing to be a living demonstration of what God can do with a small group whose trust is totally in the Lord.

During the whole of this time, we were also working to build good relationships with others in the village. There were many dogwalkers who appreciated being given free access to the parkland and woods, although a few years later we had to take special care when we also allowed a local farmer to graze sheep, both to protect them from these dogs and to help keep the front of house with the right ambiance.

Moving Forward in Faith

A great deal of practical work had already been done by the time contracts were signed, including re-roofing the centre section of the west Stable Courtyard buildings to provide the first offices, together with the upgrading of toilet and kitchen facilities. The upstairs flat over the east section of the stable courtyard, had been made habitable and occupied by dedicated long-term volunteers. All this activity had been permitted on a 'grace and favour' basis and Harvest Vision would have been legally liable to reinstate any work done on the premises if the contract negotiations had failed.

In the same period, the first of the Gatehouses was restored sufficiently to provide volunteer accommodation and Amelia Bennett, a retired missionary who on her return from overseas had not found it easy to retire and settle in this country, became our first resident hostess. She found a new call of God upon her life in caring for the volunteers and she became a blessing to many, giving us a valuable use of the Gatehouse for the future. These semi-detached cottages, on the estate but just outside the main gate, had been built by the Hospital for their groundsmen. They also provided a place for regular prayer for the small residential community who were often joined by local people.

The Bungalow and Garden Room

Having let out our home on the South Coast, we (Cliff and Monica) asked C&M Ministries to use the income we were receiving from this rental, to renovate the Bungalow and we moved in during the summer of 1996, providing bed space for any of the Ministry team who needed to stay overnight. David and Jenny Forbes regularly stayed with us from Monday to Friday each week, going back to their home in London for weekends. The Bungalow was also used for team meetings with its wood-burning stove in the lounge making it a comfortable meeting place. We were using a local architect as it had been built by the hospital for the Matron and it was not considered part of the Main House. We were preparing for our expected long-term occupancy. We had gained planning permission for an extension, so we used Bantree Buildings to design and install a portable unit on the back of the Bungalow as a temporary measure. This provided us with a dining room and two studies giving us each a quiet place for writing and study as well as somewhere for entertaining visitors on a temporary basis while we drew up further plans for its extension.

A lot of work was also done during this time to make the 'Garden Room', the only Ward now left from the hospital days, habitable. We installed a portable unit for toilets and wash basins and equipped a kitchen that made the Garden Room a self-contained unit. By the summer of 1995 heating and lighting had been installed and the whole place had been repainted inside and externally. Even the roof of this prefabricated unit had been overhauled, curtains fitted at the windows, and a large number of chairs installed for meetings and when used by local churches, or for 'away days' and prayer retreats.

Establishing a Self-Sufficient On-Site Community

The community was growing and Amelia's role as our 'House Mother' in the Gatehouse was creating a remarkable atmosphere for both long-term and casual volunteers as it also became a hub for prayer and worship that attracted people from the village and from Sandy.

In January 1995, our daughter Jenny Cooper joined the team as a volunteer. She and her husband Simon had moved to nearby St Neots in Oct 1994 to be more central for Simon's Regional responsibilities with British Telecom (and to be nearer to Simon's mother in St Ives and us). BCGA's combined office with Harvest Vision, also became Jenny's office, and she was joined by Sally Fawkes who was by this time living on-site with two young children – and her husband David was our official security officer. Between them, they organised the work of volunteers, ensuring their giftings matched with the work available.

First Off-Site Community Members

As the community increased, the number of prayer partners moving into the village and surrounding area, who were also wanting to be involved, grew steadily. Bert and Mary Godfrey, the lovely elderly couple who lived in Willington, some two miles from Moggerhanger had been part of the community from the beginning. They were lifelong stalwarts of Willington Methodist Church and had formerly owned a garage on the main road.

They remembered the war years, and we ourselves discovered many personal links with Willington.[1] Unfortunately, Bert had been involved in a road accident just outside his own home, having been struck by a neighbour's car when walking

---

1 Cliff's stepmother had been headmistress of Rye Primary School who had been evacuated to Willington at the start of the 2nd World War.

in the village. Following this they moved into a bungalow on Park Road in Moggerhanger village so that, among other things, nothing would stop them continuing to join in the community events. Mary used to push her husband in a wheelchair to join in activities at Moggerhanger Park.

They were invaluable with their good understanding of local history and later Mary used to deal with the morning post for PWM every day while Bert, from his wheelchair, took responsibility for overseeing the purchase and maintenance of the tools across the yard in the east stables area creating a workshop there. Mary's neat handwriting filled many pages of a logbook keeping a record of mail and noting gifts from prayer partners. Her careful records as well as her personal cheerfulness brightened the office each morning.

They both helped to raise money for the house when we became a collection point for wastepaper and had a skip permanently alongside the offices – we have memories of Mary in her 80s climbing into the skip and jumping up and down to ensure we had space to take more paper – raising significant sums for the work being done on the facilities being used by the Ministries. They remained part of the community for many years, always seeking to serve others. Their family also became involved in the Ministries in later years.[2]

Local Clergy Meeting

During that first year Harvest Vision organised a number of events, including a significant meeting on 15th June 1995. This was a lunch laid on by Amelia for Church leaders from Bedford and the surrounding area. About 60 ministers attended from different churches, establishing valuable links with local churches. Worship was led by the Revd Peter Eyre, a Baptist minister from Guernsey, who was staying in the Gatehouse on a working sabbatical. He

2 Their children and grandchildren figure highly in both ministries and on the site as the story develops

had done a great job in visiting the local clergy and discussing with them how they could benefit from this new resource.

More Happenings

Other significant events during the summer of 1995 were the two Bank Holiday weekends at the end of May and August which were times of worship, Bible study and community activities, with many people coming to camp out and help with the practical work on the buildings and in the grounds.

In the late Spring months, we took a phone-call from a prayer partner which appeared to be offering to provide us 'gratis' with some of our immediate needs as well as possibly those for the future from a secular source. The Swallow Hotel in Solihull was having a complete refurbishment and a local Vicar, Simon Holloway, who had the link, rang to say that we could have anything we needed for Moggerhanger House. Monica's mind flashed back twenty years to the East End of London when the Borough Finance Office had moved to another building: was God saying something? At that time, she had fitted out our NCRP Ministry offices with desks, photocopiers and other equipment. All she had to do was to mark the items she could use with a yellow cross and it was then delivered free of charge. Monica knew how to do this!

That had been a similar, but not quite the same, situation, as this time we had to provide the transport and collect it all over the first August Bank Holiday weekend that summer. But nothing ventured nothing gained! We soon had offers of vans, and drivers and volunteers to pack and unpack as well as help from Simon's church with accommodation in the vicarage, so that Monica could get in early and mark up what she felt might be needed, ahead of the vans' arrival on the Monday morning! We even had help from members of the Hotel refurbishment team themselves on the Monday to dismantle and carry down marked up items among which were bedside cabinets, wardrobes, beds, mattresses, mirrors, curtains, carpet runners - even kettles and tea making facilities. We drew the line at baths, washbasins and bathroom fittings!

Immediate storage was no problem at Moggerhanger, but the delays in the work meant that we had to store the additional beds and mattresses in Spurgeon's Homes storage depot in Sandy. Later, in fact much later, when MHPT made the decision to acquire only new furniture, even for the top-floor ministry bedrooms, the Homes gladly took them for their charity work.

The Wilberforce Factor

Research into the history of the house was still in its early stages, but we were already discovering links with the Thornton family who had owned the house in the late 18th and early 19th centuries. Godfrey and Stephen Thornton, father and son, owners of the house who had each commissioned John Soane, also had a strong family connection with William Wilberforce – he was Stephen's first cousin.

Godfrey and Stephen had links with the Clapham Group of evangelical social reformers known as the 'Clapham Sect' who were largely responsible for the abolition of the colonial slave trade and who also campaigned on behalf of those who were victims of injustice through the Industrial Revolution.

This revelation was to become very important for the Ministries as it showed the significance of the two words 'Bedford' and 'Clapham' which had been prophetically given in London when praying about the promise to give us premises for the Ministry. We were now based not in CLAPHAM but in nearby BEDFORD in a house that had generic links with CLAPHAM in south London.

The prophecy given all those years earlier was now being literally fulfilled. The promise God had given at that time was that he would *GIVE* us premises for the ministry. None of us ever thought that this would be *literally fulfilled* – that the Moggerhanger Park estate would actually be *GIVEN* to us.

God sometimes has strange ways of fulfilling his promises! But there was still much to be done and crucial decisions had to be made before we could progress further!!

An Unforeseen Interest

These historic and architectural discoveries resulted in English Heritage taking a much more pro-active interest in events at Moggerhanger. Peter's voluntary research had by now revealed that the house was the only building constructed by Soane that was capable of full restoration. Thus, English Heritage recognised the national significance of Moggerhanger Park which brought with it further delays! Their interest meant that we were no longer able to do any further work in the main house such as stripping out plumbing, and removing other installations put there during the hospital days, until English Heritage had carried out a detailed survey.

This was a mixed blessing, and it was some time before we became aware of the full significance of this survey which would change the whole direction of Moggerhanger Park and the Ministries. It took us completely by surprise to see the national interest that was growing. We had only been interested in finding a house suitable for becoming a Ministry Centre and we had found ourselves in possession of somewhere of unique architectural significance. We concluded that God must have known what was going to happen when he led us to Moggerhanger, so we simply accepted the situation and trusted God for the future.

Further Different Links

We soon discovered that English Heritage was not the only group to show an interest in this house and grounds which would, inevitably, affect in many ways what we did with it! Our visit to the Soane Museum had already introduced, or reintroduced, us to the social background of the Georgian era, as the William Hogarth satirical drawings were all also on display at that time. We intended to use these extensively when we travelled around the country recalling that period of our national history and the challenges facing Wilberforce and other Christians at that time.

We also recalled that on our first visit to view with the intent to purchase, Twigden's had told us that the Icehouse would come with the House and become our responsibility. We had not come across one before, but as we suspected it had been an early form of refrigeration used by the upper classes in their houses. It went down some distance underground and we realised it could be a hazard for young children exploring, so we needed to make it safe. We discovered that it also housed a rare breed of bats whose preservation brought further rules and the Beds Bats Society made an annual outing to check on their survival and health!

THE ICE-HOUSE AT MOGGERHANGER (DRAWING BY KATIE STANLEY)

We had a large number of volunteers in our Grounds Team including Rob and Margaret Hearing and Ingrid Coombes[3] as well as many others from the Ministries. One of our older volunteer gardeners, John Warwick, had also been a professional landscaper. He recognised that the whole estate had been designed by Humphry Repton – another name needing more investigation. In the three or four years before John and Kay, his wife, moved to Bristol, he took a special interest in identifying, and cultivating some hedging which he said would have been used all over the estate and he led our grounds team during the early years.

Building on the Discoveries

Harvest Vision Trustees saw the importance of making this extra information available to visitors from both the Ministries and increasingly wider afield. Their Secretary, Dorothy Richards, who also had writing skills,[4] set about producing a series of four-paged leaflets on John Soane and Humphry Repton and the Thornton Family. These were expanded over the years in other ways.

It was at this time too that Dorothy had had a plaque made with the 'wheatsheaf' logo of Harvest Vision and it was attached to the entrance gate where it still remains, and there was also a donated notice board erected by the first cattle grid with news and details of the on-site Ministries.

Expanding the Vision

Throughout this time, Mark Eddison, our architect, had been drawing up more plans, not only for the PWM offices, but also for the whole of the East Stables, as we were planning to provide accommodation there for a caretaker and a number

---

3 They figure highly throughout the whole story.

4 Dorothy Richards was an authority on cats and their needs, had written large coffee table books, while running a local factory for cat accessories.

of extra bedrooms for staff or visiting students, as well as the provision of possible camping facilities.

For PWM, in the first phase, unique storage was constructed in a full-length loft area above the large open room which the nurses had used as a badminton court. These plans would provide office space for other future Ministries – near the house but with independent access. The plans also provided smaller rooms on two levels with an external door which could be adapted to provide two-bedroom accommodation as a caretaker's flat.

We were also excited by the plans he had drawn up for the Main House – providing us with accommodation for a conference centre. Little did we know how long this additional planning would take to come to fruition and the further changes that would be needed to make it feasible and viable over the years.

Building Offices

At the end of June 1995 Harvest Vison had sent out tenders for the first phase of the refurbishment of the west wing of the Stable Courtyard buildings for PWM's use. This resulted in the appointment of Manor Heritage to carry out this work for the agreed sum of £40,000. The work began in July and had to be completed by the beginning of September when PWM planned to move from London. The whole of the amount needed for this refurbishment, which eventually amounted to £60,000, was raised by PWM.

Manor Heritage carried out the construction on the offices, including re-roofing, but painting inside and the outside window frames and doors was to be done by volunteers. All the work on the offices was completed by the last day of August and the volunteer decorators moved in to complete their indoor work in the next three days - just in time for PWM's office move from London.

Manor Heritage had, by that time, gained other contracts at Moggerhanger including reroofing the Main House, so they kept their site office and were prepared to move on to a new challenge of repairing the roof and carrying out the essential repairs on the Icehouse.

PWM's Move from London

On Monday 4th September the carpet tiles in the new offices were laid by a firm of Christian gypsies who used to have times of worship and Bible teaching in the Moggerhanger Village Hall and had offered their services. The next day, Tuesday 5th September 1995, PWM moved its office furniture and records from Tower Bridge Road London to Moggerhanger Park. The following day was a prayer day when staff and volunteers stopped work to praise the Lord and to intercede for the future of the new Ministry Centre for Harvest Vision, BCGA, PWM Team Ministries, and *Prophecy Today* magazine. It was a time of great rejoicing because we were beginning to see the fulfilment of God's promises.

Gatehouses Restored

By the end of 1995 the main work of initial restoration on both Gatehouses had also been completed by the Ministries, using mainly volunteers, often carried out while in residence, and providing eight bedrooms of accommodation in the two houses with further plans to unite them into one building. Although it was fairly basic, most of the donated furniture was of good quality and it would provide accommodation for a number of years for our many volunteers and visitors..

Ministry Expands

The third founding ministry, the Centre for Contemporary Ministry, had yet to move its headquarters from Bawtry Hall, where residential in-service training courses for clergy and pastoral leaders were still taking place. But with two of the Ministries now in residence at Moggerhanger we were keen to start more ministry in earnest in our new home, especially day courses

Each Saturday during September 1995 teaching days, open to the public, were held in the Garden Room starting on the theme of the Holy Spirit as already mentioned. The intention was to offer teaching and resources that were not available in local churches, but chairs still had to be borrowed from local churches and then returned, often in time for Sunday worship, but we saw this as a practical demonstration of the goodwill that had now been established.

An Unexpected Prophecy

News of these first teaching days spread far and wide, drawing more than a hundred people regularly in attendance and obviously fulfilling a hunger for studying the Hebraic roots of the Christian faith. These were very special times, which laid the foundation for the Hebraic Study Centre that would be formed by David Forbes. We always began with a time of worship and praise, and during one of these times of worship someone received a word of prophecy which was written down on a scrap of paper and handed to Cliff at the end of the meeting. After reading it, he slipped it into his Bible where it remained for a number of years, and it was only when writing up the notes for this book that we rediscovered it and noted its significance. This was the prophecy:

"My children, you will be much bigger than a relay station. You will be a transmitter!!! You will be a voice in this nation and not an echo.

My children, you have seen my handiwork at first hand, and I have built up your faith in the journey. Remember in the future, what I can do and what I will accomplish – and do not allow yourselves to be daunted by what is in hand, or by what is in the future. The hands of Zerubbabel have laid the foundations of this temple. The hands of the Lord will also complete it" (Zechariah 4:9).

It was not until much later that we recognised the full significance of this.

First Heritage Grant

In April 1995, in response to Harvest Vision's fund-raising efforts, an offer of a grant of £160,000 had been received from English Heritage to do some of the work of restoring the Main House. Harvest Vision was to continue to raise funds for further essential works, but English Heritage agreed to pay for some of the non-essential architectural works. Their offer seemed generous at first sight for which the whole community gave thanks to God, but with the continuing research of Peter Inskip and the growing interest of English Heritage, it became apparent that their intentions were for a full restoration of the house.

Harvest Vision valued all the research that Peter had carried out and had appointed Peter Inskip as historical architect to work with MEB Partnership. Mark Eddison remained our main architect even though he had originally been one of Peter's students at Cambridge!

Plans Revised Yet Again

It was at this stage that, following a great deal of prayer and discussion, the Harvest Vision trustees took an important policy decision not just to adapt the house to make it conform to our ministry needs, but to adjust our ministry needs to help with the restoration of the house. Although we had originally only wanted premises for a Ministry Centre, we believed that God had now also given to us a house of historic significance – not only of archaeological interest, but of spiritual significance due to its connection with the Clapham Sect and the abolition of the slave trade. We needed to rethink our objectives to incorporate the Ministry Centre within the context of this historic house.

This policy decision almost immediately meant that the modest sums of money which we intended to spend on adapting the house using largely voluntary labour, were quite inadequate.

Everything now had to be carried out on the historic areas in accordance with the highest standards of restoration for a Georgian mansion. The grant from English Heritage was important as, in principle, they were saying to Harvest Vision that they would be prepared to fund restoration work for a Ministry Centre that was not necessarily essentially historical but would support the ongoing life of the house.

The sum of £160,000 in the EH grant was totally inadequate for the restoration work required for the ministry in an historic house, but it was significant as a pointer to the importance of the house.

By this stage HV trustees had agreed to a phasing of the work, whereby all the outside restoration would be in Phase 1, together with some essential repairs internally, plus the repair of the historic Ice House. All of this work was legally required prior to the developers building and selling off their proposed houses.

The First Restoration Setbacks

As soon as Manor Heritage had completed the work on the Ministry offices, they moved onto the Ice House and other work that needed to be carried out funded by Harvest Vision. Our conversations with the Beds Bats Society had been important in agreeing the action we were to take – they had revealed that the bats roosting there were an endangered species and that they had also been seen occasionally nesting in the roof area of the Main House. We knew that the regulations would stop us from disturbing any who had started nesting for the whole season which could cause us further delays. We were told that noise would prevent them nesting, so we took the precaution of leaving a portable radio playing Radio 2 in the attic space while the work was going on in the Main House.

On the Ice House

While the scaffolding was being erected for Manor Heritage to start on the roof, they began to clear the area around the Ice House which had to be managed carefully as this was not too far from the cattlegrid leading to the stables where PWM were just settling into their new offices, and cars needed to be re-routed. One of the early tasks on the Ice House was the felling of a sycamore tree whose roots were damaging the brickwork.

All seemed to be progressing smoothly until a volunteer came running into Monica's office. He reported that a Tree Conservation Officer from the Council was on-site and had stopped the tree-felling and was having severe words with those who were felling the tree. She had to go out to calm the situation and mediate!! Over a cup of coffee in the offices, the Conservation Officer's attitude changed: recognition was given that the tree being felled was not a protected species as we had large numbers of sycamore saplings on the estate – but he did emphasise that *'the building firm should have known better and should have informed them of their intentions and received written permission'*. This was a conflict between the relative value and importance of buildings or trees – and one that we would meet again and again on this project – welcome to the world of negotiation and compromise! We had to keep our eyes and ears open and be aware of the priorities of others.

On the Main House

The work on the Main House also did not fare quite so well. The lead-work firm appointed as sub-contractors by Manor Heritage went into liquidation, the slate replacement team did not arrive, and although arrangements had been made with a reputable scaffolding firm, Manor Heritage themselves fell into financial difficulties and we needed to change main contractors to St Blaise, the historic building sector of Sir Robert McAlpine's.

Industrial Accident

Work on Phase 1 of the restoration of the Main House had begun in earnest on 7th September 1995 with Manor Heritage having set in motion the start of the erection of a complete scaffolding envelope around the Main House. This work was expected to take six weeks but, in the event, it took over two months and the scaffolding remained around the house for almost a year costing an eye watering £1,000 a week. The amount of money being spent on this restoration was soaring beyond all expectations.

Harvest Vision had two early-retired Qualified Surveyors among their supporters – Bob Wolton and Dennis Brown who both offered their services voluntarily – and this formed a good link between the owner and the changing client team. Dennis lived locally but agreed to come during the week to stay in the Gatehouse and became our Safety Officer and Clerk of Works.

On top of the scaffolding, a corrugated iron roof was installed covering the entire house so that the men could work in all kinds of weather. The roof required sheets of 8ft x 3ft corrugated iron in packs of 40 which were raised using a mobile crane with a 100 ft jib. During the operation, a pack dropped onto the house! Dennis caught it on film, with the crane dropping an entire pack which fell with such force that it smashed through the roof and the next two floors and even damaged the ceiling on the first floor. Despite dismay at the damage caused, there was much praising of God that our prayers for the protection of all those involved in the construction had been answered, and that no-one was hurt by this accident. The only casualty had been the portable radio which was smashed beyond repair but by this time it had successfully served its purpose!

A Further Loss

In this time of upheaval, the house experienced a further loss which worried us all for some time. A white van was seen driving off the site in broad daylight on a weekend – when there had been a number of other comings and goings. On the Monday, we found that the hardly recognisable Adam Fireplace from the main Drawing Room which opened onto the back lawn, was missing. Although immediately reported to the police, there was little chance of recovering it. It was obviously taken by someone who not only knew this site but also the antiques world – and the police considered it to be already on its way overseas to a pre-arranged new owner. Security from that time on took a higher priority and was taken to a new level.

Coming Together

By this time the community of believers was well established at Moggerhanger Park, and we were greatly encouraged by the amount of progress that had been made and the foundations of the Ministry Centre that had been laid. Prayer, Bible study and worship were at the heart of the whole work. Problems facing the Harvest Vision trustees were shared with the whole community of believers for these times of prayer, so there was a strong sense of corporate ownership of the vision – and everyone worked together with a shared purpose.

The Vision and Ethos of Moggerhanger Park

At this stage it was agreed by all to be:

• A Centre for Christians of all denominations, where they can come for prayer, study, recreation, and Christian companionship.

• A Centre known to non-Christians as a place of openness, faith, and commitment, where they are encouraged to study the word of God, and where they can see the love of Christ being expressed through words, actions, and lives.

Chapter Four

BATTLE STATIONS

In this chapter we face the biggest challenge to our faith we have so far encountered when the Developers try to build bigger houses. We face losing the house and everything we have invested. We address the Planning Committee, and the Developers appeal to the Secretary of State for the Environment and threaten us with eviction.

1996 – A Year of Hope

We did see 1996 as entering a year of hope even though, just before we closed the offices for Christmas 1995, our electricity supply failed and we had a two-day power cut over the whole site, preventing us holding any Christmas celebrations, but we had had promises from the Electricity Board to prioritise upgrading the overall system in the New Year.

So, 1996, after all, *DID* begin as a year of great hope in expectation of considerable progress with the restoration of the Main House. The offices on the west side of the Stable Courtyard had been successfully completed, PWM had taken up residence, and work was now focusing on restoring the Main House roof and other essential work that needed doing. We, and our growing community at Moggerhanger were excited by the interest that English Heritage was taking in the house and their promise of grant aid. The downside was that they were demanding a considerably higher standard than had been originally envisaged.

Roofing Delays

One example of this was, that having erected the scaffolding reasonably easily, with just that one scary incident, we could have repaired the roof quite quickly by simply replacing faulty slates. English Heritage, however, insisted on stripping the entire roof and getting rid of all the Welsh slates which had been used for repairs during its hospital days. These were to be replaced with Westmoreland slates of the same genre as those used by Soane in 1791. These were eventually found in a job lot coming from the demolition of the Manchester Mental Institution, but the delay was a warning of things to come.

Work on the external walls, windows, roof, and stonework continued throughout the year. The work was now being carried out to a very high standard by St Blaise, the historic building sector of Sir Robert McAlpine's. It was hoped that they would have finished the work by Christmas 1996, but it too dragged on, and it was New Year 1997 before even the scaffolding was removed.

More Good News!

The sheep brought in by the neighbouring sheep farmer to graze on the front lawn in an effort to regain the ambiance of the estate, were back after a winter away while the scaffolding was erected – this time with their lambs. They gave a feeling of new life to all who visited at this time as well as to the staff. PWM had settled down well and the additional desks they now needed had been donated by Mid Beds Health Authority as being 'surplus to their requirements'. The wide number of local contacts we had involved was paying off.

Dorothy was delighted with the responses to the 1995 Christmas card with a picture of the House, which had been produced and used in various mailings and soon added notelets and postcards to the resources on offer to visitors who continued to drop in to see what was happening. 'Friends of the Park' was also formed by Harvest Vision to help practically and financially during the year initially with 50 regular supporters taking out standing orders and this grew rapidly.

Consolidating the Community Activities

Having more people on-site during office hours, had meant a further look at cooperative arrangements and the contractual division between the roles of employed staff and volunteers. Little did we know how important this would become in the future.

One minor early hitch was in the collection and sorting of the post which had always been a voluntary role each day carried out from the Gatehouse, but PWM had their own structures and rules in place which needed to be settled amicably. The adjoining 'Well Room' became the Mail Room and changed its function whenever this was needed – never being used as an office but often used for storage.

Jenny's role expanded and the concept of a 'House Committee', which had worked so well when we were in the East End of London, was expanded at various levels combining the management of overall activities with business events. Until this point, Simon had worked alongside Jenny in his spare time, but in August 1996 he took a voluntary redundancy package from his job with BT which enabled him to work full time in a voluntary capacity at Moggerhanger. Bringing his business skills, he assisted Jenny in coordinating the start of the transfer of CCM activities from Bawtry to Moggerhanger and developed community relationships with the local community by becoming a governor of the local school, as well as building relationships with local churches.

Joint Events

The daily courses and other concepts such as Leadership Days and the Monthly 'Saturday Nights at the Park' got under way and were a great success. The foundational work for a Hebraic Study Centre began to be thought through, later to be renamed 'Pardes'[1] literally 'Garden' and being distinguished biblically as more of a 'Garden of Eden' than the more formal 'Garden of Gethsemane'.

---

1 The Hebraic Study Centre started as a series of teaching correspondence courses.

We adjusted to having Ministry staff on-site for set hours alongside those volunteers who came in as, and when, needed. The first Bonfire Night with PWM on-site was a great time of cooperation; this meant that the Gardening Team gathered appropriate timber and delayed lighting the Bonfire until after office hours, when the PWM staff could bring their families (and fireworks) to join in the fun. The Thursday Lunchtimes became Fellowship Lunches where each one brought what they had to share and ate together when we were also able to share news and highlights - as well as problems (the cold winter spell had not only highlighted the electricity problems but also those with the heating). The piping from the boiler to the new offices had to be rapidly dealt with – it had not been included in the renovations!! Joint Open Days were agreed and planned for 20th July and 21st September in addition to individual Ministry Annual Gatherings.

Further Resources

The Garden Room was fitted out with practical gifts of crockery and cutlery and continued to be used on a self-catering basis by the Local Churches for PCCs, Quiet Days, Alpha Courses and even an Open-Air Eucharist took place for 10 local churches on 1st September.

During the early months, thought was given to more forth-coming needs of the growing numbers of young people and it was agreed to set aside an area and prepare a proper camping ground behind the Garden Room. Help came from our new local farming friends who carried out the necessary harrowing and we did manage to hold a memorable Open Youth Camping event on the weekend of 12th-14th July.

Sharing The Vision

St Blaise, our contractors for this stage, were very cooperative and Dennis Brown, our Harvest Vision-appointed voluntary Clerk of Works, was able to keep a full record of works as they were carried out including many photographs. The week before Easter, while the scaffolding was still up, we were able to offer a very successful guided tour of the house. Six or seven levels of walkways had been agreed and cordoned off and hard hats, which Dennis had obtained, were compulsory. Seventeen different craftsmen came in specially and could be seen carrying out lead working, timber replacement, slating, repairing coping stones, stonework, replacing window frames etc and they also loved showing off and discussing their work. The Ministries were developing a good relationship with the specialised workforces.

Celebrations and Widening the Vision Further

On March 8th which was the first Anniversary of the signing over of the House to Harvest Vision, we had celebrated with a cake, and during that time of thanksgiving the news came in that English Heritage had paid some of the grant into our account at the same time as the first repayment of VAT we had applied for had also reached the bank!

On March 28th Sir David Money-Coutts held a well-attended Reception in Coutts Bank in the Strand, London emphasising his own family banking links with the Thornton family. An Exhibition on the House had been prepared which stood in the Bank foyer for a number of weeks and was then transferred to the Bank of England for display there before coming back to Moggerhanger. Discussions had been going on at this time for a possible Christian School of Business Ethics to be based at Moggerhanger.

On May 19th our nearest neighbour, Sir Sam Whitbread, Lord Lieutenant of Bedfordshire, hosted a reception at Moggerhanger for local dignitaries and businessmen who were then able to have a short tour of the house. At that time too, Peter Inskip had published a significant article on the architecture of Moggerhanger House in 'Country Life'.

Delays and Possibilities

While things were moving forward well in the Ministries, the whole restoration project was becoming increasingly expensive, and we had a strong feeling that everything was steadily being taken out of the control of our little community and we were gradually being forced into something we had not foreseen. Originally, we had only wanted a ministry base with reasonable accommodation and teaching facilities, but we were now being forced to take responsibility for an historic house and all the accompanying hazards. The work now envisaged could no longer be completed by the end of 1996 as we had anticipated.

Additionally, the whole project was now not only beyond the capacity of Harvest Vision to fund, but English Heritage (EH) also said it was beyond their capacity too. They therefore recommended an approach to the National Heritage Memorial Fund (NHMF), a Government body that had been in existence since the end of World War II for the restoration of important heritage sites. EH promised their full co-operation with an application and so too did Peter Inskip, who was now also one of the Fund's architectural advisers.

An approach to the NHMF in December 1996 produced an encouraging response following which the HV Trustees asked Peter to prepare an application. This brought to an end any hope of completing even the external work in the spring of 1997 while an application was being considered. We and the community prayed much before submitting the application and we concluded that the renovations would bring the house favourably to the notice of a much wider public who would wish to visit. This would give us the opportunity of sharing our faith with others whom we could not reach through our own work.

Mixed Warnings and Blessings

In May 1996 the English Heritage Committee made a visit to Moggerhanger House and in July the Mid-Beds District

Council, together with their senior officers, also paid an official visit. A number of different trusts had given small grants to Harvest Vision during the year, but money was always tight with spiralling costs on the restoration work. Every month all those involved with us in the Ministries and community, regularly got before the Lord to pray for the money immediately needed to meet the outstanding bills. The amazing thing was that, month by month, just sufficient money *DID* come in to meet our obligations and not once did Harvest Vision go into overdraft at the bank.

Storm Clouds Gather

There were, however, other clouds on the horizon that became darker and more threatening. In January 1996 the developers, now Kier rather than Twigden Homes, applied for an enhancement of their planning permission for 12 houses. They had decided that the profit margin was not sufficient to make their small houses profitable, so their architects had now designed considerably enlarged properties with six bedrooms on two floors each with three integral garages and many other features. This was a far cry from the original modest single-story houses agreed when we purchased the Main House and 15 acres.

Enhancement Opposed

We felt we had no alternative but to oppose these plans as two of the houses would be in full view of the Main House and detract from it, and others would encroach into the woods as well as breach the historic walls of the Walled Gardens.

We could see that these large houses would have a negative impact on the Main House and its estate. We told the local Parish Council what was happening, and they too opposed the application with a large amount of support from the village residents who realised that the free access to the parkland and woods, that they (and dog walkers) presently enjoyed, was also at risk.

Developers' Anger

Mid-Beds Planning Committee duly refused planning permission for this enhancement. The consequences for Harvest Vision were severe. The Developers were extremely angry with the Charity and told us that they would modify their plans and reapply later in 1997. They warned us that there would be severe repercussions on the Charity if there were any further objections on our part. They still had considerable power over Harvest Vision as we had already overrun the timetable originally agreed for the completion of the essential repair work on the house, due to the intervention of English Heritage.

Moreover, the Developers had also retained a charge on the Gatehouses, the Bungalow, and the Stable Courtyard buildings which we had purchased at the same time as the House – in a separate deal with Twigden, which had been in the package they had passed on to Kier. They told us, in no uncertain terms, that if we opposed their revised planning application they would not only foreclose on these properties and repossess them, but they would also repossess Moggerhanger House and the Bungalow where we were living!

A Difficult Decision

Whether or not to continue opposing the enhanced planning application was a desperately difficult decision. If we did not oppose, and the proposed huge houses were built, the whole ethos of Moggerhanger Park as a place of peace and tranquillity for ministry as well as retaining its historical significance would be destroyed – but if we opposed and they foreclosed on us, we would lose everything. It appeared that whatever decision we took, we could only lose. We needed a miracle!

That, for all the community at Moggerhanger, was a challenge for prayer. For us personally, there was not only the threat of losing everything that we and our Prayer Partners had invested in the House, but we would also be homeless!. We were no longer renting out our house near Rye in East Sussex. It had already been sold and we intended moving our furniture into the Bungalow on the estate in the summer months.

Battle Begins

We sent urgent calls to our supporters asking for prayer. Many of them came to Moggerhanger and joined us in Prayer Walks. The Darmstadt Sisters of Mary were magnificent. From their base in Radlett Hertfordshire, they came to Moggerhanger bringing about 50 small flags, each bearing a Scripture verse. Armed with these, our community walked around the entire estate covering with prayer every part of the grounds including the woodland, the walled gardens, and the old orchard area.

We especially, concentrated on those parts where the proposed houses were to be built. The Lord had told us that 'the houses would never be built' so we had to be especially careful in waiting upon him for the strategy that he would use to prevent them being built. It also meant that we had to take a huge leap of faith in opposing the Developers at the hearing of the Council Planning Committee.

To Oppose or Not

The Harvest Vision Trustees did not find it easy to come to a joint decision to oppose the Developers, and even the Chairman thought we should not oppose them. They were afraid of losing everything that they had gained thus far. We, Monica and Cliff, had to work very hard to secure any kind of decision to oppose, pointing out that we not only had everything to lose in terms of the Ministries that we led, to which many of our supporters had contributed financially, but also the home we had been preparing for the next stage in our life, as our children were now independent. (Unbeknown even to our own family, we had put most of any life savings that we had at that time into Moggerhanger Park).

We personally had more to lose than anyone, which was as it should be, since we were the leaders of the project. None of our community knew to what extent, but we daily spread all the issues before the Lord who knew everything about us. To our dismay some of our fellow trustees thought that the possibility of losing Moggerhanger House was too great a risk to take, and that we should no longer actively oppose the building of the houses.

About a week before the application was due to go before the Planning Committee, we were alerted to a commotion outside and going out to check, we saw a JCB being driven towards the Walled Gardens. It went just beyond the walls to the area that used to be the orchard and the driver began digging a large hole. When this was done the JCB left the estate. We were puzzled; until someone pointed out that the Developers were probably planning to say to the Planning Committee that they had already started building the houses by digging the foundations. The pressures upon us intensified, and our prayers became all the more urgent.

The Planning Committee Meeting

The application was due to go before the Mid-Beds Planning Committee on 26th November 1996. But this was deferred for a 'site inspection' by members of that Committee. The issue came back to the Planning Committee two weeks later, on 10th December 1996. Our Chairman had declared his intention of attending and submitting to the demands of the Developers in order not to put at risk everything we had already invested in the House. But he was taken sick on the day of the meeting, and he was unable to attend. We took this as a sign from the Lord that we should attend the Planning Committee and take his place knowing that he would have said that we had no objection to the application. There was no time to consult the trustees, so we had to take any decisions ourselves as an act of faith, but we only did so on the word of the Lord that the threats of the enemy would not prevail. So we went to the meeting to speak on behalf of Harvest Vision – not without some fear and trepidation!

We both attended and on our arrival at the Town Hall, we were dismayed to read in the notes set out for the meeting that despite strong objections from English Heritage, the Parish Council, the Georgian Society and Peter Inskip on behalf of NHMF, the Mid Beds Council Planning Officer had submitted to the committee a report which was strongly favourable to the Developers. In his report he was recommending that approval should be given for the enhanced development. The report stated:

"Planning permission now already exists for 12 dwellings on this site as an enabling development package to secure the refurbishment of Park House. The applicants, who originally owned all of the site, sold the house to Harvest Vision for a fairly nominal sum and at the same time created a fund to assist in the refurbishment of the house which the new occupiers could draw from. The work on refurbishing the house is now well advanced and the enabling fund has been nearly used up. It must be emphasised that it would not now be reasonable to object to the principle of allowing new housing to be developed within the grounds of Park House."

False Information

We suddenly realised what was happening. This information given to the Planning Committee in this report was both inaccurate and misleading. The phrase saying that the Developers had *"created a fund to assist in the refurbishment of the house which the new occupiers could draw from"* was quite untrue. It gave the impression that the Developers were pouring money into the refurbishment of the house, and they had nearly used up this 'enabling fund' that they had set up. It made the case for them that they now required the enhanced value of the enabling development from these 12 houses in order to complete the restoration of Park House! It was quite likely that the Planning Committee would have accepted all this and the enlarged houses would have been built.

All of this was totally false, as the Developers had not put a single extra penny into the refurbishment fund. The whole of the £350,000 for that purpose in that separate bank account had been raised by Harvest Vision! The bank account was in the name of Harvest Vision, and it was composed entirely of our money. The Developers had only insisted on being one of the signatories to ensure that the cheques drawn on this account were used for the essential repairs. Harvest Vision had raised separately, funds for the scaffolding, roof repairs and much more. It appeared to us that the officer had been "taken to lunch" by the Developers who had given him all this false information and he had not taken the trouble to visit us, to consult us, or to check on its accuracy.

Harvest Vision was allowed only three minutes at the Planning Committee hearing in which to lodge its verbal objection and Cliff used the time just to draw attention to this inaccurate information. Unfortunately, the Officer who had written the report had temporarily left the meeting during Cliff's statement on behalf of Harvest Vision, so he did not know that the accuracy of his statement had been challenged. Upon his return, he was asked to comment, and he merely affirmed that what he had written in the report was true without going into any details. He thus unwittingly called into question the truthfulness of the statement Cliff had made on behalf of Harvest Vision.

Planning Committee Decision

Despite the false information given to the Planning Committee, the members evidently believed Cliff, rather than their own Officer. They *unanimously* refused the application, thus going against the advice of their Officer. This was a remarkable decision since a unanimous vote of the committee, which included members from all three political parties, rarely occurred. We saw this as divine intervention. Only God could have united the minds of each one of that committee and caused them to reject the recommendation from their own Officer who had made a powerful case on behalf of the Developers!

The Developers had employed a barrister to present their case to the committee in which he had contradicted Cliff's statement. We saw this as further evidence that we were involved in an immense spiritual battle in which we had been assured by God that the battle was his, so that truth would inevitably prevail.

After the meeting there were strong words from the Officer concerned against Cliff as the representative of Harvest Vision. The Chief Planning Officer, however, had been present throughout the meeting and the following morning, he visited Moggerhanger Park and personally apologised unconditionally for the behaviour of his staff. He recognised that his Planning Officer had not presented a truthful picture to the committee, and he promised to write a letter, not just to the Planning Committee, but to all Members of the Council, correcting the false information given in the report. This was very welcome news and a great comfort to us to know that the Chief Planning Officer was supportive of our case. Now we had to await the wrath of the Developers.

The Developers' Attack

The reaction of the Developers following the decision of the Planning Committee, was swift and angry! They immediately appealed to the Secretary of State for the Environment against the decision of Mid-Beds District Council, but they also now turned the full force of their venom against Harvest Vision.

Chapter Five
1997: A Year of Uncertainty and Change

This is an exciting chapter as although PWM, the second of the founding ministries, was now settling in and the united ministry and community activities developing well – the overall venture was under threat and might not survive. We record some of the most difficult decisions we had to face, but prayer and faith triumph. Through yet another Moggerhanger miracle, God provides the answer, but even so, the battle continues.

Foreclosure Imminent

It was rather disturbing that we had discovered Moggerhanger four years ago and it had 'belonged' to us for three years, but by the beginning of 1997 the Developers had officially given Harvest Vision Trust 90 days' notice of their intention to foreclose on the properties. Once again it appeared that we were about to lose everything. Only divine intervention could save us from disaster!

The Developers, when they had sold the property to us had included a clause which created and held a charge on the property and one of the requirements was that we should complete the essential repairs within one year so that they could build their houses and make the money that they so greatly coveted.

Due to all the delays caused by English Heritage's intervention to ensure that as much of the historic house could be retained as possible, these repairs had not as yet been completed. Of course, this was not our fault. We had not asked English Heritage to become involved, but the Developers were in no mood to exercise mercy. We were now facing their full wrath.

We knew that if they went to law, they would have a powerful case as Harvest Vision had clearly failed to complete the essential repairs in the legally agreed time, although, of course, it was due to circumstances beyond our control. Whether or not this would count in a court of law was arguable and we knew that we were now facing the loss of, not only our Ministry base, but the whole of Moggerhanger Park including our own home in the Bungalow – and including everything that we and our prayer partners had invested in the project.

Other Action Taken

As part of their vengeance against us, the Developers then refused to sign cheques on the special Harvest Vision account containing not only the money we had provided for the repairs in the first place (which were held in a restricted fund) but also for other grants we had been receiving, to carry out the work. This meant that the contractors could not be paid for work which they had already carried out and for which an architect's certificate had been issued. It was clearly the Developers' intention to embarrass Harvest Vision and to disturb our relationships with those who were doing the work of restoration.

This placed us in a difficult position with the contractors who needed the money to pay their workmen which then also increased our own separate cash flow problems, but this was all part of the battle. We recognised that this was further evidence of the intensive spiritual battle that was raging over the house which God had provided as a place of special significance for the Kingdom.

Urgent Prayer

We began 1997 with a series of urgent prayer meetings and crisis consultations of the Harvest Vision trustees. Following the Council meeting which had rejected the enhanced planning permission application, our Chairman had resigned and there was considerable nervousness among the remaining Trustees. Would they all walk away from the project leaving us alone, because of the stand we had taken on drawing the attention of the Council to the error?

We had been so sure that the Lord had told us that the Developers' houses would not be built that although we had not exactly gone against our chairman and trustees and opposed the Developers enhanced application, we had not given in as he would have done. Harvest Vision now faced a legal battle with the Developers and we recognised that the whole project would only prevail through prayer. We put the community on battle alert and informed our prayer supporters throughout the land of the situation facing us, calling for their urgent prayers. Then we organised more prayer walks around the grounds as the whole community responded to the battle alert which lasted right through from January until August when the appeal was to be heard.

Kier made one important concession. They suspended the 90 days-notice of foreclosure until after the hearing of their appeal, for which they engaged top London lawyers.

A Cooperative Effort

The appeal was set for 24th - 26th August 1997 and greatly to our joy, the Mid-Beds District Council took responsibility for preparing the legal case against the Developers in defence of their decision to refuse the enhancement submission for planning permission for those much larger houses.

Harvest Vision Trustees were now fully supportive of the stand we had taken. Cliff and our Ministry staff and the Mid-Beds District Council Officers and their staff spent a great deal of time in preparing the case for an objection. The Council set aside Officers to work with us in preparing the papers and legal briefing. The spirit of cooperation and working together blessed everyone in many different ways, and this was to stand us in good stead in the future through the good relationships we had built up with the Council Officers.

Preparations for the Future

Harvest Vision also independently set about tightening up its structures and policies. This meant expanding the number of its Trustees including inviting David Saunderson, a committed Christian, well-qualified accountant and City businessman with local connections, to become both a Trustee and Treasurer. He set about establishing further contracts for the work.

Harvest Vision discussed and approved the appointment of Patrons and Advisors, and we established great relationships with many influential people who lived locally including Betty Barrance MBE representing Moggerhanger Parish Council who opened many doors to the local community.

The original Harvest Vision Trust Deed with its Memoranda and Articles was legally reworded to ensure that control of buildings was included and it, along with the production of the Harvest Vision Seal at the same time, is now kept in a safe place! By June the Trustees were also discussing a proposal of a way in which Harvest Vision's name could be changed to embrace becoming a Preservation Trust.

An agreement and partnership were made with CCM Trustees so that CCM immediately became the active arm in running Moggerhanger Park through a subdivision called 'The Park'. CCM officially took over this responsibility for running The Park on 1st August 1997 and Simon and Jenny Cooper became its leaders. They had been carrying out the role anyway while had they were living on Simon's redundancy money, but within a year the Jerusalem Trust started to provide two years of initial 'seed-money' for this new role, a new Company structure was set up for 'The Park' and a degree of independence was built in for operating the Park sponsored and underwritten by CCM.

Site Planning

One of the advantages that came out of the electricity failure before Christmas had been that British Telecom had come back with a firm offer of £15 per telephone line attached to our own on-site network exchange. We needed to plan carefully for the future and immediately took out 7 consecutive numbers and set up a contract with Chiltern Telecom for an internal switchboard system.

A number of queries had also arisen over the Bungalow: one was its conspicuous nature as it was in full view of the historic house – and seemingly quite out of character. Although still furnished with odd furniture, it was already proving an invaluable resource for us as well as for our ministry leaders such as David and Jenny Forbes from PWM, who needed accommodation. We noted that it had been built in the 1920s for the Hospital Matron so we were following tradition in providing accommodation for on-site leaders!

In an effort to solve a number of seemingly potential problems we considered re-siting the Bungalow alongside the Gatehouse complex, plans for which were also being drawn up by Mark and being considered at the same time. But we also agreed that we ourselves would take personal responsibility through C&M Ministries, for funding a new self-build Potton style house. In the event, all plans for the Gatehouses, Bungalow, and Orangery were put on hold while further funding was being sought.

Further questions on the Bungalow were then raised on the validity, as Trustees of Harvest Vision, of our benefiting from living on-site rent-free even though we had used our own money for the Bungalow renovations, so we backdated an agreed rental payment against the conversion costs and ceased making independent improvements. This did mean though, that there was now no question of allowing us to purchase this property separately from the estate as we could have done if we had bought it straight from the Developers. From this time, we gave up our dream of being totally involved for life, and recognised that we would need eventually to live off-site and also plan for a future beyond our direct involvement – we were in it for the long term!!

Community Changing News

Those who were at the core of the resident on-site community were also changing, a number had served voluntarily for three or four years and were on the move and their places were being taken by others. Of the three stalwarts in from the beginning, Brian Privett who had brought with him such excellent plumbing and building experience at just the right-time, had tried to move out locally to provide a home for his family, but then had moved back to Oxfordshire when they did not settle: Mike Baker moved away for a short while to caretake a local community centre in Bedford but kept in touch and returned to help out a number of times as we will see later in the story – and he was still assisting the Ministries ten years later with his, at that time unknown, computer skills.

Towards the end of 1996, Sally and David moved their personal home from Skegness and bought a house locally in the village, David, having served the community in a voluntary capacity for four years, went back into secular work. Sally stayed involved for many more years in the Ministries and then went on to use her nursing background to pioneer Community nursing locally but staying in touch with the Harvest Vision community. David's security role was then taken over by Meg and Tom Howse, who moved into the stable accommodation that the Fawkes family had vacated. Within a year they too had moved on and we were recruiting others to carry out vital roles.

Amelia Bennett had been the first 'House Mother' in the Gatehouse and remained the continuing linking factor for a number more years. David Forbes had been Cliff's right-hand man in PWM in London, having retired early from his executive role in BBC publications and he became the key person for coordinating all Ministry activities, But more changed plans were imminent as he and Jenny, who was also a national Lydia leader, never did make their house-move up to Moggerhanger from London. While they were making their plans, David was diagnosed with cancer and although they commuted for a while using their own room in the Bungalow, his last days were spent at his home in London – he passed away on Good Friday 1997 – a great loss to Cliff and PWM, the Community, and the Biblical and Hebraic Study Centre for which he had had the vision. He had also given 'Pardes' its name as a 'Planting of the Lord'.

Community Action

There was aways plenty of practical work to be carried out by the increasing number of both skilled and unskilled short-term volunteers – on the grounds and in maintenance and general estate work as well as with the Ministries on their various mailings and other activities, but also guiding tours in the Main House and with all the repairing and and fresh modernising opportunities on the estate. English Heritage gave permission at last to continue stripping out the central heating pipes installed by the hospital. The drive had deteriorated and was in a terrible state to welcome visitors – CCM organised some temporary repairs as well as creating underground channels to link the electricity supply separately between the Bungalow, and the Gatehouses to the central meter reading building now situated behind the Stable-Courtyard buildings.

Strangely, in July – our monthly reckoning of accounts showed an unusually large claiming of Volunteers' Travel Allowances. Investigations found that these were being recycled as gifts to cover the purchase of a chainsaw to make things easier for the growing work being carried out by Volunteers in the woods and they were also being taken and returned as donations towards the T-shirts and Sweatshirts to provide the Volunteer team with identifiable uniforms. The team were gelling together in new ways under Jenny and Simon's leadership and they wore them whenever on duty. When open to the public, the recognisable dress with the 'Park Tree' symbol on was used by those acting as guides and on Open Days! The 'Park Ministries' now had an identifiable presence with a regular printed news update at the centre of the work.

A very healthy relationship had also grown up between all the Ministries – one of the memorable roles Simon was drawn into, was the 'goodbye' ceremonies to any leaving staff or volunteer member. His literary gifts and understanding of the Ministries led to constant demand for a 'leaving poem' – in fact it was maintained that Esther McLachlan returned for a second stint of employment in a new capacity mainly in order to receive another poem! Life was always interesting, creative, and all-embracing even though the future had a sense of uncertainty.

Research Findings

Then Peter, in his historical architectural research, discovered that the Kitchen Pavilion, previously thought to have been a Victorian addition, was in fact an original feature by Soane. Although planning permission for its demolition had been obtained by Twigden during the period when it was owned by the Developers, it had never been carried out. The Ministries had been relying upon this information to enable them to demolish the internal walls and convert it into an 'assembly hall' that would have seated about 150. This research discovery was a severe blow to our Ministry plans, and we began to see the link between Peter and English Heritage as a threat to our hopes of using the house as a Ministry Centre.

But a month or so later, our hopes rose again when Peter made a further discovery that there were the foundations for an Orangery just south of the Stable Courtyard – and Mark worked with Peter on planning a building on that foundation which might be able to fulfil a Ministry purpose, as it was large enough to double-up as a meeting hall for 200. We saw this as a divine provision and as justifying the decisions we had taken, and that in time this would be built.

On a positive side we then discovered that David Fawkes, one of our earliest volunteers who in 1995 was still living on-site as our warden and security officer with his wife and two young boys, had photography skills among his other gifts and he went round with Peter filming and recording the areas that we could not normally reach – so that we had videos to share with our prayer partners – and also to use for necessary fundraising.

Peter Inskip, our Historic Architect, promoted Moggerhanger House in his circles and the Architectural Summer School, run by the Attingham Trust, who were visiting architectural significant buildings round the country on a three-week tour, chose to visit us in 1997. Peter's research in the archives in the Soane Museum, revealed that Soane had not only built the Main House, but he had also designed all the Stable Courtyard buildings where our Ministry offices were located and that he had even designed the walls of the Kitchen Gardens.

This Stable Block finding precipitated more work on the MOUs (Memorandums of Understanding) between the Ministries in the administration of their office occupancy of these, but the Walled Garden discovery was of great significance in the legal case being presented by Mid-Beds Council and Harvest Vision. It meant that we were able to claim that building the houses, by breaching the Walled Gardens, would destroy a part of the unique historical architecture of Moggerhanger Park.

English Heritage, for their part, responded to this news in May 1997 by listing the Walled Gardens, woodland, parkland, and the surrounding farmland, which used to be part of the estate, and including them in their 'Register of Parks and Gardens of Special Historic Interest in England', Grade Two. All this helped with the case against the Developers.

Upgrading the House – and the Cost

Then the following month, June 1997, the Department of National Heritage took the next step and upgraded Moggerhanger House itself to Grade One. This was on the grounds that the house was discovered to be the last remaining country house designed by Sir John Soane that was capable of full restoration. The fact that the House was now Grade One listed and the grounds were registered Grade Two, greatly strengthened the case against the building of houses in the grounds that were in close proximity to the house. The upgrade had a further benefit and also meant that we were now eligible for major grants from public funds.

But, inevitably, there also a cost! In order to facilitate this major national upgrade to Grade One, the Harvest Vision Trustees were advised that it was necessary to establish a distinctive 'Preservation Trust' as the Harvest

Vision Trust Deed, although now amended considerably, was primarily concerned with Christian evangelism which did not sufficiently include any restoration of an historic building. This news was greeted by Harvest Vision as being both good and bad.

The Trustees needed time to think and to pray about the decisions they would have to take for the future of the whole Moggerhanger Park project which was changing from the provision of an old house for ministry purposes to the restoration of a national treasure of historic significance which could be used for ministry. How could the two contrasting objectives work in harmony? The decision to create a new Preservation Trust was deferred until the results of the Appeal were known.

The Decision

The Developers took us right to the wire. It was just a few days before the hearing was due to be heard in London on 24th August 1997, when the lawyers acting on behalf of Kier, notified Mid-Beds District Council of their intention to withdraw their appeal. They had evidently concluded that the legal evidence against them was overwhelming, and they had no chance of winning, especially now that the house was Grade One listed.

The news was conveyed to us at Moggerhanger Park by the Chief Executive and the Chief Planning Officer both of whom were quite jubilant. Our joy was overwhelming, and we immediately set about informing all our Moggerhanger community and our supporters throughout the country who had been faithful in prayer. We wanted them to know that this was another 'Moggerhanger Miracle'. It was indeed a spiritual battle that God had won, and we wanted to give all the glory to him!

More Crucial Decisions

Although the Appeal to the Secretary of State for the Environment to reverse the decision of the Planning Committee had not been allowed, so that the enhanced development was no longer a threat, the battle with the developers was still raging.

There was no end in sight. Harvest Vision did not 'own' the land where the proposed houses were to have been built, and the planning permission for twelve small houses was still in place. The Developers could still defy the council and build their smaller houses – there was nothing to stop them, although we all knew that economically it would be disastrous for them.

The Trustees were now called upon to make a series of further decisions that would affect the whole future of the House and the Ministries at Moggerhanger. We were desperately in need of the Lord to show us the way ahead. Harvest Vision Trustees spent many hours in discussion and prayer while considering the decisions that still lay ahead.

Furniture – More Provision

As if to challenge our faith, it was in August that we then had another approach from the Swallow Hotel chain, using the link we had established in Solihull, with the offer, in their Refurbishment Programme, of more furniture from another hotel and this time with even greater cooperation in delivering all that we might need. Now that the pressure had been lifted, Dorothy was able to respond positively as she knew the kind of furniture that would be available and its quality. She returned a full list of our requirements for up to 80 bedrooms including those rooms intended in the new structures not as yet built.

Another Difficult Decision

The immediate celebrations following the withdrawal of the Developers' appeal to the Secretary of State for the Environment were once again short-lived. Within days we were plunged into a period of intensely difficult negotiations on several different but related issues.

The Trustees of Harvest Vision had originally accepted the recommendation of English Heritage to apply to the National Heritage Memorial Fund (NHMF) for assistance. As the house was now listed Grade One, English Heritage estimated that the restoration needed a major grant that was beyond the capacity of their own funds.

This application to the NHMF had been favourably received, but by this time a major part of the NHMF's funds was coming from the new 'National Lottery' and was being administered by the newly established Heritage Lottery Fund. Harvest Vision was faced with a further difficult decision. As a Christian charity, the majority of its supporters and all its trustees had an aversion to the lottery. The trustees were therefore faced with a moral dilemma over whether or not to accept the major grant from the National Heritage Memorial Fund if it were to come from this new source. We could not have been the only ones as the NHMF recognised the difficulty faced by some Christians and this appeared to be solved as HLF ruled that they were making provision for churches and Christian organisations to receive their grants directly from the Treasury.

Justifying the Answers

This seemed good to Harvest Vision Trustees and after a great deal of soul-searching it was resolved by the recognition that God had provided us with an historic building which clearly had a unique value in the nation and would be opened to the public as well as being used for ministry. Clearly God is never taken by surprise, and he knew what he was leading us into. It was therefore justifiable to accept money from the nation for the restoration of a national treasure that was entrusted to our care and provided for our use. This was a decision taken jointly by the Trustees of Harvest Vision and all those involved in the Ministries which included the Moggerhanger community.

Harvest Vision Trustees continued seeking the Lord for several months before finally taking the decision to establish the 'Moggerhanger House Preservation Trust' to own, restore, and maintain the property for the Ministries. They saw the involvement of English Heritage as a positive asset for the Ministry believing that God had given us a house of national importance for a purpose. Its *spiritual heritage*, linked with the Wilberforce connection, as well as its architectural importance, would enhance its Ministry.

It was reasoned that English Heritage would give publicity to the house bringing many visitors who would be interested in its history. This would then give Ministry staff the opportunity to speak about the work of the Clapham Group and its links with our own work today, which would give natural opportunities for sharing our faith and speaking about the gospel. We saw this as an amazing strategy of evangelism which was all part of God's gift of a unique Ministry Centre.

We will turn now to a chapter on the Developers' next actions before we describe arrangements for establishing MHPT to carry out this role.

Chapter Six
A NEW WAY FORWARD OPENS UP

This is another exciting chapter where we record some of the most difficult decisions we have to face, but in spite of these, prayer and faith triumph. Although the battle to prevent the houses being built was now won, we did not own the land on which they were to have been built. Through yet another Moggerhanger miracle, God provides the answer.

By this time English Heritage had become committed to the full restoration of the house and, on Peter Inskip's initiative, the process was begun for obtaining from them a major grant. After months of discussions with the National Heritage Memorial Fund, we were told in July 1997, just one month before the Appeal which could allow or prevent a total foreclosure on the whole estate, that a grant of £3 million had been approved 'in principle'. This was conditional upon our obtaining the freehold of the walled gardens and preventing the Developers from building their proposed 12 houses, whatever size, on the estate.

The Appeal

In the previous chapter we recounted how we had redoubled our prayer coverage of the estate as the hearing of the Appeal drew near that the Developers had lodged with the Secretary of State. The upgrading of the house to Grade One and the listing of the grounds as being of historic interest must have been a severe blow to the Developers. We also had all the evidence to show that they had not contributed to the 'restoration fund' but had just used the money we had provided and thus their motive in building the houses was purely for commercial gain. Their lawyers would have known all this, which is probably why they withdrew their Appeal just one week before it was due to be heard. They knew that theirs was a hopeless cause. It looked as though at last we were through that battle.

Back to the Developers

The planning permission to build twelve modest-sized houses, though, still stood and had not been revoked. If Keir did build these, it would not only destroy our hopes for the whole estate, but also, we would now lose the £3 million restoration grant promised by the National Heritage Memorial Fund. It was at this stage in August 1997, once the Developers had dropped their Appeal, knowing that they were still very sore and blamed Harvest Vision (and particularly Cliff) for having to do this, that it was agreed that Cliff should make contact directly with the Keir directors, who were still using the name of Twigden Homes, on behalf of Harvest Vision to ascertain what their intentions were for the future.

The Developers prevaricated but said they would be willing to sell the land to us, but that they would want a sum in excess of £2 million. We consulted the District Valuer who valued the land at between £1.0 million and 1.2 million. But raising even such a sum as this seemed totally beyond our ability. We went back to prayer, seeking guidance for the next step. It was at this stage that we heard of a new 'Landfill Tax' in Bedfordshire from which grants were available for local charities.

The Landfill Tax

On hearing mention of this New Tax and knowing that Moggerhanger might be within the beneficial area, Cliff immediately sought a meeting with the Chief Executive and Chief Planning Officer of Mid-Beds District Council, both of whom we knew were committed Christians and who had recently been so helpful.

Cliff said that he had heard reports of a new 'Landfill Tax' and asked if it were possible for us to benefit? They both began laughing and then explained that the Chief Executive was the Secretary of a Steering Committee that had been set up to deal with the organisation and distribution of this new 'Landfill Tax' which had been established but not yet implemented. All the information was readily available, but they had so far not done anything about it. It was so complex that they did not think it would be possible to set up the necessary infrastructure before the first application, on which there were limiting time constraints, could be even considered.

Nevertheless, they told us all we needed to know. The Landfill Tax had only been instituted the previous year in the last months of John Major's Conservative Government, and now there was a new Government led by Tony Blair. The tax was to be collected by the Customs and Excise on every ton of rubbish brought out of London and some of this was being dumped into the old sites of the London Brick Company near Bedford.

Thousands of tons a day were being deposited there by Shanks & McEwan, and a small part of the tax on this could be given to local charities within ten miles of the landfill sites. To qualify for a grant the charities had to be one of 'religious', 'environmental projects', or engaged in the 'restoration of historic buildings'. We were about eight miles from the nearest site, and we qualified on all the conditions! But it was not all good news.

Setting up the Structure

As we knew, nothing had so far been done in Bedfordshire to set up the necessary structure to handle the tax and if it were not claimed by the end of September 1997, it would automatically revert to the Treasury. It was now well into August, so once again we were confronted with an almost impossible situation, and it looked as though we were about to see a possibility drop away from our grasp.

We Needed Another Miracle – In Fact More than One!

Following urgent talks with the Chief Executive and with others on Bedfordshire County Council, they agreed to set up a small team of officers charged with the responsibility for setting up an 'Environmental Body' in Bedfordshire 'EB Beds' and for helping Harvest Vision to prepare an application. The willingness of the Council to cooperate with us yet again, we saw as another case of divine intervention that would not have happened if we had not stood firmly against the Developers and Cliff had not spoken at the Planning Committee meeting on behalf of Harvest Vision.

A further 'small miracle' resulted in a successful appeal to the Customs and Excise which gained a 'one-month' extension; so, we had until the end of October (now less than two months away) to put in a claim on the grant from the tax. Together, we managed it and in the end there were only four valid applications in the county of Bedfordshire, and it was known that about £3 million was available representing a whole year's tax waiting to be distributed.

The Steering Committee met on 9th September 1997 and along with a number of smaller grants, allocated a grant to Harvest Vision of £1.2 million for the freehold acquisition of the 15 acres of land, including the walled gardens, held by Twigden Homes.

Then came the problem of persuading the Developers to accept that amount – well short of the £2 million they had requested! We all knew that yet another miracle was needed, so the praying community at Moggerhanger went into action. We spread the whole issue before the Lord in times of worship and thanksgiving for all God's goodness to us in the past and we looked to the future with confidence that he would find some way of fulfilling his promise that those houses would now never be built.

More on Landfill

Immediately, another small miracle happened. It was recalled that the Landfill Tax had been one of the last things established by the Conservative Government before being replaced by Tony Blair's Labour Government. The initiator of the new tax had been Sir Nicholas Lyell QC MP who was now on the opposition benches. He was still the MP for Bedfordshire North, but he had been the Attorney General responsible for drawing up the legal framework of the Landfill Tax grants for ensuring that local charities benefited from it! Cliff immediately made contact with him and explained the situation.

The Chief Executive of Mid-Beds District Council was also a personal friend of Sir Nicholas and they both agreed to meet the Developers and to negotiate on behalf of Harvest Vision. Following a difficult meeting, agreement was reached. We rejoiced greatly and thanked God for yet another amazing answer to prayer.

But, even so, the battle was by no means over; in fact, our faith was about to undergo the most severe test of all.

Shanks & McEwan

The regulations governing the landfill grants said that 90 percent of the grant was to be paid from the tax and 10 percent had to come as a direct gift from the landfill operator. A spokesman for Shanks & McEwan phoned and spoke to Cliff saying that it was going to cost his firm £120,000 for us to have our grant and it would be cheaper for them to let the tax money go back into the Treasury. He said that if we wanted to make sure of our £1.2 million, we should send a gift of £120,000 to his firm!

This was shattering news! *We were stunned!* Cliff, who had taken personal charge of all the negotiations, responded, saying that we were just a small Christian charity, and we did not have that sort of money. Cliff also reminded their spokesman that, as a registered charity, it would not be legal for us to give gifts to individuals or firms. The spokesman said that he knew all that, but it would have to be paid through a third party. He said, *"If you want to be sure of your grant, I need a letter from you and Harvest Vision promising a gift to my firm of £120,000".* He said that how we found and paid the money was our problem! We could pay it through a third party.

We checked with the Customs and Excise who confirmed that this request was perfectly legal. Moreover, looked at dispassionately, there was no reason why a commercial firm should make a gift to an unknown charity in order to help them to obtain a Government grant. None of the Shanks & McEwan directors had any knowledge of our work. It looked as though, once again, we were likely to lose everything that had been gained. We needed another miracle.

A Testing 24 Hours

The HV Trustees had a testing 24 hours, conferring by phone. It was a time of getting before the Lord for guidance. For the sake of £120,000, which we could borrow from the bank or from individual donors, were we prepared to put the entire project at risk which now included the major grant for the house? The Trustees all felt that this was a test of our faith in God therefore the answer was an emphatic: 'Yes!' God had brought us thus far and he would not forsake us. Our trust was in the Lord. But the Trustees all left the final decision to Cliff, which was an enormous responsibility.

Cliff and Monica spent a lot of time in prayer seeking guidance from God. There was something about this whole demand for money just in order to pay it to a secular firm, that did not seem right. We did not feel that the Lord would lead us to do this sort of deal, especially after the amazing things that had happened to bring us to this point.

We also did not believe it would be right to try to borrow money from the bank. In fact, we saw this whole situation as a test of our faith. Did we now have the faith to put our trust totally and completely in God? We had to say 'Yes' to this. But it was not without considerable fear and trembling that Cliff wrote a letter stating firmly that we would *NOT* be sending the requested 'gift' as we did not feel it was right.

More Good News

It was some three weeks later (a very long 3 weeks indeed!) before we heard from Shanks and McEwan stating that they were prepared to make a gift of £120,000 to Harvest Vision enabling us to claim the Landfill Tax Grant. Unbeknown to us, Sir Nicholas Lyell had been in touch with the chairman and directors of Shanks & McEwan, and he had been influential in interceding with them on our behalf. But by now it was mid-October and if the money were not paid by the end of October, it would automatically go back into the Treasury.

We had lots more work to do to ensure that we met the deadline but first we had to give thanks to God, knowing that it was his intervention that had saved the situation. It was clearly the Lord who had prompted Nicholas Lyell to intervene on our behalf as none of us in Harvest Vision had got those connections with industry, and none of us had asked him to intervene on our behalf. Once more God had done something amazing to enable Moggerhanger Park to become a living reality. We shared the good news with our own little praying community and later with the wider company of supporters telling them of the graciousness of our God who never makes a promise without fulfilling it.

Eleventh Hour Decision

It was 4.00 p.m. on Friday 31st October 1997 – the last day for the grant – that we received a phone call from Customs and Excise saying that all our papers were in order, and we had qualified for the money. At five minutes to 5.00 p.m. that same-day, formal notification was faxed into our office that the money had been paid into our bank! We were able to make out a cheque for the full amount and hand deliver it to Kier that Friday evening. We did have a last-minute problem as Cliff did not put enough '0's in writing a cheque for £1,200,000 – he had never handled so much money before and was clearly suffering from stress in the course of the whole event! The Developers made a considerable fuss about losing interest over the weekend while this was being rectified – but the deal was accomplished. And Simon had the joy of correctly making out a cheque for £1,200,000 and delivering it by hand to the Developers on the Monday morning.

Prophecy Fulfilled

We expressed our gratitude to God in prayer; but we also warmly thanked the chairman and directors of Shanks & McEwan whose generosity had enabled us to receive the £1.2 million grant from the Landfill Tax. With this money Harvest Vision was able to pay Keir (Twigden Homes) and receive the freehold of the 15 acres of agricultural land and woods that they had withheld from the original contract.

Now that we owned the full estate that had been the hospital, we were able to ask the Mid-Beds District Council to rescind the planning permission for the 12 houses, and thus Moggerhanger Park was secured for all time. The word of the Lord that Cliff had received on that first visit to Moggerhanger Park – more than four years earlier in August 1993 – *"Those houses will never be built"* was at last fulfilled; and the word of God was proved once again to be faithful. This was just one more in the list of the many 'Moggerhanger Miracles'.

Chapter Seven
1998 AND THE FORMATION OF A PRESERVATION TRUST

This chapter sees the setting up of Moggerhanger House Preservation Trust. Also Thornton Family links are discovered, and another major grant is secured. Other major contributions are made, and organisational procedures are established.

Making 'Fit for Purpose'

While the momentous action in 1997 had been taking place, other things had also been under way following PWM and CCM's arrival. Harvest Vision had been carrying responsibilities for the house plus the estate since the early part of 1997. They had also tightened their Trust deed and made it more 'fit for purpose'. None of this was wasted but all was found to have a different relevancy when, at the end of the year, the decision was taken that a Preservation Trust should be formed as an entirely independent entity. **It was always envisaged that the Ministries would take back responsibility for the house once it had been restored, so that a Ministry Centre would remain the major objective.**

Also, it was never the intention of Harvest Vision that a Preservation Trust would be responsible for operating the house as a Christian Ministry Centre. In order to guarantee this, the Trustees asked the lawyers to ensure that these objectives were written into the Trust deeds, so that the house and estate would always be used for Christian Ministry.

This took many months to accomplish with lengthy consultations between lawyers and other advisers. It was not until the following year, 1998, that Moggerhanger House

Preservation Trust (MHPT) was formally established as a registered charity alongside a charitable company with limited liability. One important step taken, was that MHPT as a Charitable Trust whose major object was the restoration of Moggerhanger House, would have only one Member – Harvest Vision. In this way, the power of ownership of Moggerhanger Park would always be held in the hands of Harvest Vision in order to ensure that its Christian objectives were met in the formation of a Ministry Centre and its future use.

Forming a New Trust

Although by September 1997 Harvest Vision had carried out the preparatory work and set up most of the initial arrangements for MHPT, with itself as the only Member, MHPT was not expected to take responsibility for the full restoration of Moggerhanger Park and its estate until the following year 1998. Relationships were important, especially as Harvest Vision and the on-site ministries were to carry on operating the events at Moggerhanger with all their volunteers. It was further agreed that CCM would create a new department called 'The Park' to work with, as well as alongside, its educational work.

This was the department that would coordinate, and oversee, all activities as the ministries developed and Simon Cooper had been appointed Centre Manager with Jenny working closely with him. They were both already well established with the local community, so they set about developing further links with the village, building up a large team of volunteers (both local and from further afield) who would help run the regular programme of public events on the estate. This was intended to leave MHPT free to concentrate on their sole purpose of restoring the buildings – finding the relevant funding for specific renovations to preserve the historic nature of the building and also setting up a 'Sinking Fund' for sustainability to cover future maintenance and caring for the estate.

Initial MHPT Trustees

The initial MHPT Trustees had been drawn from those of Harvest Vision especially those who had some experience of administering buildings. The initial six Trustees were three with business experience at various levels, Peter West (chairman), Andrew Ingrey-Senn and Dorothy Richards (Secretary), then there was David Saunderson who had City financial experience and the two of us, Cliff and Monica: Monica had rather different practical experience as she had successfully renovated and brought back into use, four redundant churches in their ten years in the East End of London and had successfully rebuilt one.

At the recommendation of HLF, before MHPT was fully set up to start to hold meetings, three more Trustees who had some experience of listed properties and who could also understand what HLF's requirements would be, were drawn in. We already knew each of these – one of whom was Sam Whitbread, who was still on the Board of Whitbread plc and who owned the nearest large estate to the south of Moggerhanger which he was running as Whitbread Farms. He was known to HLF to be a good businessman and could handle appropriately large sums of money. He was also Lord Lieutenant of Bedfordshire and church warden of a local Anglican church and had several other parish churches under his patronage. The other two Trustees we also knew and had already been working with them – they were Helen Dorey, Assistant Curator at the Soane Museum in London with historical architectural experience and Henry Clarke, Company Director of Crown Estates who was one of our prayer partners with experience of several other Christian trusts and their properties.

Unfortunately, our nine trustees had been reduced to eight by the time we were fully registered in January 1998 as Peter West, our first chairman of Harvest Vision, felt now he also needed to resign from MHPT.

Bringing in the Thornton Link

The Harvest Vision Trustees had been researching the links with the Thornton family, owners of the property for 100 years from 1750. Monica had been searching for descendants – some individuals and couples had come on a day visit in October when they had had a conducted tour of the House with a promise that they would be one of the first to be invited to stay when the restoration was completed. Sam Whitbread had entertained them to a meal at the adjoining Southill Park.

The Thornton family were bankers and both Godfrey and Stephen had been Governors of the Bank of England. They had commissioned the alterations by Sir John Soane. We had good memories of being received positively in the City the previous year when we had produced a display exhibition of facts and photos at Coutts Bank in 1996 and had then followed this with a series on Business Ethics in the Garden Room.

Peter West, our chairman, had enthusiastically formed the 'Thornton Institute of Business Ethics' in London with its own seal, registering it in his own name and also incorporating the family logo without first getting the current family's permission. This was not viewed favourably by some of the incoming trustees, and in January 1998, Peter stood down as both Chairman and as a Trustee. His departure was a considerable loss to the community as he had been one of the original visionaries and Chairman of Harvest Vision for the first few years. We were sad to lose Peter. The role of MHPT Chairman was then taken by Andrew Ingrey-Senn, a local businessman, who had also been one of the founding members of the praying community and a prime mover in setting up the original Harvest Vision Trust which he was also chairing. He carried the role of Chairman of both trusts for some time.

Adding Advisors

We also had a number of other supporters who preferred to serve as Advisors rather than Trustees and were willing to be involved on specific issues. In January 1998 to mark the launch of MHPT, Dorothy, our secretary of both HV and MHPT, produced an 8-page booklet with photos and people descriptions of those who were either Trustees or had accepted the role of Advisor and were on our Advisory Council at that date. She added this to our growing number of resources which we made widely available to local people, interested Trusts and our Prayer Partners.

This Advisory Council were prominent active supporters: Bedfordshire County Councillor John E Scott, Mid Bedfordshire District Councillor Caroline Montilla, and Moggerhanger Parish Councillor Mrs Betty Barrance ensured good local involvement. Also involved were Timothy Knox, architectural historian to the National Trust, Dr Stephen Parissien, of the Paul Mellon Centre for Studies in British Art in London, and part of Yale University, Neil Burton of the Georgian Group, Patrick Bowring from Sotheby's and Peter Inskip – our historical architect also represented the Royal Institute of British Architects.

Trustees Structural Planning

The first MHPT Trustees meeting was held at Moggerhanger Park on the morning of 23rd January 1998 followed later in the day by a meeting of the Advisory Council. They were now not only making plans for the restoration using the Soane plans for the Main House, with the £3 million grant from NHMF which had been given for the internal renovations – and these were also necessary for making it into a Ministry Centre, but now in addition to the original House and surrounding area, a further 12 acres of the estate had been recently added. Although this came debt-free it came without any continuing funding support.

This new acquisition included the historic Walled Gardens which Humphry Repton had designed, so the new Trust were also making plans to follow the designs laid out in Repton's Red Book of 1792 and its 1798 supplement.

The Trustees immediately put in place a Finance Committee of which Cliff was a member. They also set up a Landscape Committee and a House Furnishings Committee both of which Monica was a member. The latter would also embrace the rapidly growing Library facility of books for courses – many of which had already come from Bawtry Hall ahead of CCM's forthcoming move. This was greatly supplemented by BCGA's move of books from Scotland at the start of 1998. These were all being held for sorting and cataloguing by the Ministries in the far end of the Garden Room.

During the early days in 1998, the new MHPT Trustees met with the Ministry Trustees to understand the background and events at Moggerhanger that had taken place in the last 5 years and joined in where possible with the other activities. They worked closely with CCM who were carrying out the operation of the site using 'The Park' community. This was still being coordinated by Simon and Jenny Cooper and very soon Simon was also assisting MHPT by preparing their Business Plans and helping them in other ways.

MHPT then started to produce their own MHPT newsletters with the first one dated January 1998 which also offered copies of a Video of the external restoration of the House which David Fawkes had filmed with Peter Inskip and was now being commercially produced.

Problems with Transfers

The transfer of property and assets from Harvest Vision to Moggerhanger House Preservation Trust did not go particularly easily. Legally it was found to be difficult, and to no one's advantage, to value the House itself at the price Harvest

Vison had paid – i.e. £1 - and this was raised to £1,000,000. Additionally, we were advised that it needed to include the safe-guarding of the rights of the initiating ministries whose prayer partners had provided the original restricted funds and should be correctly worded in case there were problems in the future with the inevitable change of Trustees. It was formally agreed that *'The Ministry expectations should always be kept as a foremost priority and passed on from Harvest Vision to MHPT.'*

In the end the Transfer of the Walled Garden contract was eventually signed in London with Bates, Wells and Braithwaite acting for MHPT on 2nd April but not until registration for VAT had also been successfully put into operation.

Further Trustee Expansion

By March 1998, when more additions and amendments were made to the Trustees as HLF (on behalf of NHMF) continued to make more recommendations, we also approached both Richard Bisgrove, Horticultural University Lecturer with grounds experience, and Isabelle Errol, the wife of Lord Errol, hereditary Lord High Constable of Scotland, who farmed a neighbouring estate which was on the Sandy ridge on our eastern side. We had just discovered that Isabelle had links on her side of the family with the Astell family who had married into the Thorntons – the family who had owned the estate in the 19th century. This seemed so naturally right to ensure that our 'neighbours' on each side were fully involved, so we now had 10 Trustees to carry MHPT forward although even more changes would be made in the next two or three years.

Celebration of the Latest Acquisition

It was actually not until the 22nd of May 1998 that the Mid-Beds District Council and the Bedfordshire County Council together with the then newly formed Board of Trustees of 'Moggerhanger House Preservation Trust' all met with the

Directors of Shanks & McEwan (Southern Waste Services) and held a joint celebration for the Acquisition of the Walled Gardens by Moggerhanger Park. This was held at Moggerhanger, and we rented a marquee for the occasion and provided a nice lunch which gave us a good opportunity for making our witness and telling them all how our faith in God had been vindicated as he had provided for each step of the journey from giving us Moggerhanger House for £1.00 through to their generous gift that had enabled us to purchase the woodland and the rest of the estate. We remember that at that time this still had planning permission for houses that would now never be built. God had fulfilled the promises he had made.

The programme for the event stated –

Our celebration today marks two events. We are commemorating the fact that the walled gardens and woodlands historically associated with Moggerhanger House have been acquired and preserved for the benefit of the village, the county, and the nation as a whole. We also mark the start of the project to restore these grounds to their original design. We hope you enjoy our celebrations today and we are excited by the prospect of the house and grounds being returned to their former splendour, and open to the public.

It was not long before this group of committed MHPT Trustees were holding early morning breakfast meetings each month at Moggerhanger and they soon started functioning more fully by drawing others onto sub-committees.

The new Trustees were each making their own personal contributions to the project and were particularly interested in improving the general ambiance of the house and the impression given to visitors when first entering the estate. In the early days we had used sheep to keep the grass on the front lawn under control and it was thought we might be able to continue this policy and introduce special breeds.

The new Trustees also agreed that the Bungalow could become quite an eyesore because it had not been there in the 18th century but it had been specifically built for the Matron when it had become a hospital and was permanently in the line of vision from the front of the Main House. We were pleased that some thought had already been given to its possible relocation alongside the Gatehouses out of direct view.

Possibility of Further Expansion?

The Mid Beds Council were being very cooperative and were interested in the plans we had, not only for moving the Bungalow mentioned above but also for Mark's plans for expanding the Gatehouse to be a full Visitor Centre at the entrance to the whole estate and extending the volunteer accommodation this would provide to help with its maintenance.

Mid Beds Council went even further and alerted us to the possibility of cooperation on other farmland they owned in Moggerhanger. Although the neighbouring Park Farm, leased to our friendly farming neighbour, Keith Peacock, still had five years to run, he had intimated his intention of relinquishing a large adjoining barn back to the Council which we felt might be suitable for conversion into staff and further volunteers' accommodation at the right time. This seemed to be a good proposal and could help with further servicing Moggerhanger Park. So in January our architect Mark Eddison's early outline plans for renewing the Stable Block complex to serve this much needed purpose were put on hold until possibly later in the overall programme when further changes would be needed and they could be accomplished together.

Growing Park Activities in 1998

The newly formed Operating Group, now led by Simon and Jenny, built on and formalised more of the 'Park' operations programme. They formed smaller groups and started to produce regular mailings to keep everyone in touch.

A Ministry Open Day in June was run successfully as a Family Day closely followed in July by an open outdoor Youth Concert held as part of **a** Youth Camping Weekend for local churches.

Regular activities continued and expanded throughout the year such as Teaching days, Prayer days and Fellowship lunches all in the Garden Room. The previous year, the Ministries had commissioned, and paid for, a new toilet block from Bantree Buildings at the entrance to the Garden Room.

This facility enabled the use of double the number of loos available on-site – much needed for the National Heritage Open Day on 12th September. This was the first time we had participated, and we opened just for the afternoon which attracted over 500 people. A printed programme was produced, and three timed short tours of the house were offered gratis. There was also a Garden Trail, an area for Craft and other stalls, and an Historical Photographic exhibition in the Garden Room as well as refreshments.

Although the intention of the National Heritage Open Days was to open up historic buildings free of charge during these weekends, it was possible to make a small charge for three bookable-in-advance illustrated talks in the Drawing Room – which we made accessible through the French windows from the back lawn. Helen Dorey gave the first of these on 'John Soane', Peter Inskip gave one on 'Moggerhanger House' and Dorothy Richards gave the one on 'Grounds and the Family' and places were soon fully booked for all three. The accounts showed that in total over £1,000 was added to the Operating funds from that single event without making access charges!.

It was around this time that we applied for, and obtained, a brown sign on the Bedford Road directing strangers to the entrance to Moggerhanger Park – we were becoming known more widely.

Security preparations also took place at The Park in October for our first Royal Visitor and the Duke of Gloucester visited on the morning of the 3ʳᵈ November 1998 when a buffet lunch was prepared to follow a conducted tour of the now accessible, although still beng worked upon, Main House.

Ministry Specials Join In

Two weeks after celebrating the Acquisition in June when access to the House was still limited, PWM had held its own Open Day in the Garden Room, majoring on its newest publication *Roots and Branches*. This was an exploration into the Hebraic background of the Christian Faith by a number of prominent thinkers and writers as a commemoration of David Forbes and the part he had played in establishing the teaching of the Hebraic Centre. His successor Dr Walter Riggans was introduced as PWM's Deputy Director and further day courses for Hebraic Studies were soon added.

A Family Resources Day was held in October coming out of the Parliamentary work. Much of the research was coordinated by CCM in the Garden Room and also in other venues in Bedford.

On 27ᵗʰ October Helen Dorey hosted an evening reception at the Soane Museum in London which introduced that facility to others at Moggerhanger while also opening up other supporters to the Moggerhanger project.

The long-term regular fellowship gathering Bonfire Night took place on the 7ᵗʰ November but now becoming a full Fireworks display with invitations extended to the whole village and large crowds attending.

The Christmas celebrations took the form of an all-inclusive Christmas party on the evening of the last day that the offices were open, with a Christmas lunch provided by Amelia for the staff before they closed for a full two weeks: new traditions were being established!

Relevant Futher Ministry News

Prayer Expansion. 1998 had been a busy year for the newly appointed MHPT Trustees and for the CCM Park Operations team whose numbers were swelled when Gillian Orpin returned to live locally. Gillian, who had been very much involved with the ministry in her Deanshanger deaconess days, had taken some years out to care for her mother as she had been rapidly losing her sight and living alone in a remote area on the edge of a loch in Scotland. We had kept in touch and visited her during that time. While there she had been ordained in Oban Cathedral as the first woman Anglican Minister in Scotland. She was to prove a blessing in many ways and began to run regular prayer days as well as organising daily prayer for the whole site.

Parliamentary Action. The Parliamentary Report that Cliff had been working on with MPs and peers for more than a year, was presented to Jack Straw, the Home Secretary in the Moses Room of the House of Lords on 15th July 1998 with much allied publicity. Two years later the 'Family Matters Institute' would be formed as another member of the Moggerhanger Ministries.

Crime Intervenes. The new Operators suffered their first break-in in May and the loss of their expensive sit-on mower which they had only purchased the previous year with a special donation. It had been kept under lock and key, nothing else was disturbed and only the one item was missing, so the police, having commended them on their security precautions, concluded that it must have been carefully timed and taken by someone who knew the security arrangements and where everything was kept. At the time, there were few outside volunteers on-site and even the Bungalow was once again unoccupied as Cliff and Monica were taking a party to Israel. The insurance paid for a replacement mower but for some time to come, the Gardening team had a policy which varied where they kept it.

Books and More Books. The Church Growth Book Service had been based at St Ninians in Scotland for 7 or 8 years and was now planned to come to Moggerhanger. Friendly officers from the Salvation Army driving down from Crieff delivered all the boxes the day before the offices reopened at the start of the year 1998! Fortunately, there were already volunteers staying in the Gatehouse and the books were transported to the storage space at the far end of the Garden Room as BCGA were still sharing their small central office with Harvest Vision.

Many of these books would become part of the Moggerhanger Library as soon as the World Mission Library set up for the CCM courses was also transferred from Bawtry Hall lter that year. Lynne Wortley had been our CCM Administrator at Bawtry Hall from its start and she had been carrying out her duties alongside training for the Anglican Ministry. Jenny, who had been a teacher for a number of years, had been appointed by CCM to oversee and coordinate any future courses from a Moggerhanger base taking over Lyn's responsibilities when the move of CCM to Moggerhanger was finally made in 1999.

Attempting Residential Courses

The first of the local 4-day residential courses for church leaders was held at Kings Park in Northampton on the 26th – 29th January 1998 in cooperation with the BCGA on '*Natural Church Development*'. This was a new concept of church growth concentrating on the health of the church, and had ben developed with Christian Schwarz from Germany on one of Monica's visits there when she was President of the European Church Growth Association. Monica had worked with Christian and overseen the English version of both the hard-cover Handbook and the accompanying Manual and she was already carrying out several personalised research surveys throughout the British Isles.

The Manual was just back from the printers and we were working on several smaller booklets highlighting different dimensions as well as producing videos on characteristics such as *Need-Oriented Evangelism*', one of the 'Healthy Church Characteristics'. A number of further 4-day courses on this subject, for clergy, were held in June and October. These were now all being held at Moggerhanger as the resources were set out and easily accessible, but accommodation was booked in the Sandy Travelodge and local volunteers were opening up their homes to host the delegates. Hope was strong that soon fully residential courses would be able to be held at Moggerhanger.

Regrouping BCGA

Early in the year BCGA suddenly lost the services of Sheila Collins who developed a serious heart condition. She had been their secretary since 1993. She was admitted to hospital in February, and we then had a number of temporary secretaries for short periods while BCGA regrouped its central operations. Richard Quennell had become Book Manager in 1998 and in 2000 when Dr Philip Walker having moved his home from York to live locally had joined Monica in the growing work, the BCGA offices moved into the East courtyard first floor flat as it was no longer needed for housing on-site staff.

More Problems Looming on the Horizon

Things did not go smoothly for MHPT. English Heritage visited in July 1998 to talk through the major grant Harvest Vision had been offered and negotiations with HLF were very slow and more problems came to the fore.

On the positive side, during September John Phibbs, noted garden historian and part of the Debois Landscape Group, had also visited. The Trustees were discovering more about the leading 18th Century landscape designer Humphry Repton and John was able to help. He later became Principal of DLG and was awarded an MBE for his research. DLG Debois Landscape Survey Group became fully involved with us.

It was 18th September 1998, before MHPT received a signed contract for the grant that would take us to the next stage. But even this did not stop the problems – read more of other problems in the next chapter.

Chapter Eight
WORKING WITH THE HERITAGE LOTTERY FUND

Slow progress is made with this major grant. New architectural discoveries bring more problems and more delays. We encounter many difficulties during this period of the restoration of the house.

The new group of now 10 committed MHPT Trustees at the start of 1998 had begun negotiations with HLF confident that the agreement reached with Harvest Vision and all the promises previously made to that trust, would be honoured. We were aware that in accepting money from HLF, we were also making commitments to open the estate to the public. This was something we were very happy to do and identified a number of people already known to us who had architectural and landscape knowledge as well as experience in managing a country estate.

Sadly, though, the attitude of the HLF staff from the beginning seemed to be one of constant suspicion and non-co-operation (occasionally bordering upon hostility), alongside a constant moving of the goalposts. It was distressing at the time, and it was only much later that we recognised that they too were still in the early days of establishing their own existence and identity, and drawing up their own operational guidelines. We, ourselves, had managed to clear all the hoops but the huge sum we had at last been granted, must have been seen as an enormous responsibility to them and they did not want to make any mistakes.

Conditions Imposed by HLF

At this point, HLF started imposing more conditions upon MHPT including putting forward the names of even more trustees. Harvest Vision had already anticipated this and had put it into MHPT's deeds that all Trustees should not only be committed Christians but should also be required to sign the Evangelical Alliance Statement of Faith. Sam Whitbread was one of the first Trustees in this new batch who had already expressed some reservations about the statement as he was not from that strand of Christianity. Cliff offered to help in resolving any difficulties and he took his Bible and went and spent a morning with him which evidently helped as an agreement was reached.

We had originally suspected that the difficulties we faced with HLF staff must be because we were known to be Christians, although later we heard of other projects where the organisers were treated in a similar manner, so we were forced to the conclusion that this was the current *modus operandi* of the HLF regime, and in order to progress we needed to be able to 'tick all their boxes' which changed at each stage of the work.

We had ensured, to the best of our ability, that the new MHPT Trustees were all people with high professional qualifications and experience, who were used to working in a context of professional integrity. It was, though, not easy for them to adjust to working with an organisation that seemed to them to be sometimes amateurish and incompetent as well as authoritarian. To them the staff of the newly formed HLF appeared incapable of understanding the complexities of restoring a Grade One listed Georgian mansion. Every piece of information was treated with suspicion and in their eyes, we had not yet fully proved ourselves as being capable of handling large sums of money.

In the previous chapter we reported that one of the conditions that had been attached to the promised £3.0m grant was that the houses for which planning permission had been given 'should never be built'. The only way this could be achieved was through our gaining ownership of the land and, at the time that the promised grant was made, this seemed highly unlikely to anyone outside of the Moggerhanger community – probably including HLF. In fact, we were probably the only ones who believed that it WAS possible to stop those houses from being built.

It later became apparent that the HLF staff too had not thought that we would ever be able to fulfil all the conditions they had imposed and so would NOT claim the grant which we think must have been the largest they had offered anyone at that time in their short history. It had been promised in July 1997 and there appeared to be astonishment when we came back only four months later saying that we had succeeded in securing the land. This news was greeted with almost incredulity.

Our joy gradually turned sour as every possible objection and imaginable obstacle seemed to be then thrown in the way. We had not kept it a secret, so HLF knew that the ultimate objective of the project was not simply the restoration of a Georgian mansion and opening it to the public, but that its use would also be as a residential Christian Centre. Of course, they accepted that the end-use of the house would be important for the future maintenance of the building, so the viability of our plans for the Christian Ministry Centre was of considerable interest to them.

In addition, they would ask (sometimes seemingly 'demand') to see every detail of the plans and viability for bedrooms and conference accommodation and also the projections for the operation of the centre including expected income and expenditure. It became abundantly clear from the attitude of the HLF staff that this was a project that was considered not viable and we were going to have to exercise considerable diplomacy and patience if we were to succeed in carrying out the planned restoration with their support. Some of our Trustees now questioned whether their support was even desirable.

Broken Agreements

Andrew Ingrey-Senn, MHPT's second Chairman, a businessman with considerable managerial experience, bore the brunt of negotiations in which one agreement after another was broken. The rules were constantly changed, and additional conditions were laid down. Internal staff changes in HLF added further complications as newly appointed officers rarely honoured agreements made by those they succeeded, or they claimed a lack of documentary proof and challenged MHPT to prove that such an agreement had even been reached.

When written documents were supplied demonstrating the agreement that had been reached, it was dismissed as no longer relevant. It also became clear that the HLF staff believed that, as a little Christian charity, we were bound to fail. They told us that many other charities like ours had failed to deliver and they clearly had no confidence in our ability to break the mould.

Lengthy Delays

It was this constant changing of the baseline by the HLF staff that made negotiations extremely difficult. More importantly it created lengthy delays. This had two major effects.

The first was that costs soared, as with any building works subject to considerable inflation at that time.

The second effect was that many of the subcontractors, and professionals with whom MHPT were dealing, lost confidence in the ability of the Trust to maintain the momentum. Often this made relationships difficult to handle when HLF delayed payment for work that had been done.

Members of the professional team, in particular, became extremely frustrated by the lengthy negotiations and the additional work they were required to do in order to justify each particular part of the project – which of course always increased costs. The gross prevarications of the HLF staff made the work almost impossible to achieve and these additional costs were never reflected in an increase to the awarded grant. That was fixed for all time, despite numerous new discoveries of additional architectural gems which required additional work and also additional costs incurred, just by the lengthening of the time it took to achieve.

There was a third effect – that of bringing the Ministries, who had already raised considerable sums of money to get the work to this stage, much more into the picture. The recently formed MHPT Financial Team began to see the need to fundraise not just from those agencies and trusts willing to support buildings, but also from those willing to support Christian action. This needed to be done in partnership as it had already been agreed that CCM when they moved from Bawtry Hall would eventually be the lead Ministry, operating the ministry as well as managing the opening of the buildings to the public and the CCM trustees were prepared to amend their own Trust deed at the right time. The Jerusalem Trust had not long given CCM two years 'seed money' to employ Simon to carry out this role of coordinating the use of Moggerhanger while making it clear that they could not support the renovation of the buildings in any way themselves.

The HLF grant conditions had made it necessary for Harvest Vision eventually to make the ownership of the buildings over to MHPT, so Simon was, therefore working closely with MHPT trustees to draw up their business plans and even took over taking the minutes of their meetings. After around a year of the operating grant it was discovered that any trading carried out operating the Park needed to be fully part of the MHPT business plan and directly accountable to MHPT, so CCM, after much consultation, made over the remainder of the grant to sustain Simon in this role while he continued to work towards making Park Ministries self-sufficient.

Getting Beyond Stage One

The Restoration had been planned to be carried out in stages – and we were still only part way into Stage 1 which we had always expected would be completed in a limited timeframe, so that we could move on to other even more complex developments, but it was dragging on and on.

Essentially, there had to be a considerable degree of flexibility built into a complex restoration project in which on-going research was revealing more of Soane's unique architecture all the time. Inevitably, each new find required some change to the plans and an adjustment for its inclusion as the House was stripped and Soane's plans and notes were subjected to a minute scrutiny. Although HLF were enthusiastic and desirous of the work on the new discoveries being carried out to the highest of standards, the size of the grant could not be increased to match the extra work and improvements being made. This created tension all round and difficulties in relationships. Although the amount of the grant could not be increased, neither could the original schedule which affected everyone.

This caused enormous frustration in the professional team that we had appointed, who objected to their judgements on budget priorities being challenged. The HLF staff admitted that they had been given limited powers of discretion to cope with such a project and often the changes necessitated by new discoveries during the progress of the work had to be referred back to the trustees of the National Heritage Memorial Fund. They were the ones who had awarded the original grant of which the HLF were only intended to be the supervisors. This entailed more months of tedious negotiations, more delays, more inflation, more costs, and less benefit from the grant as it was never adjusted to meet the changing circumstances.

In the light of these frustrations, we decided that the best way to counter the attitude of HLF was to show them that it was possible to combine the opening of the estate to the public with the professional operation of a Christian Centre. If fact, rather than being a problem, we felt that this could be a God-given opportunity to show that Kingdom principles really worked. Simon was already working closely with MHPT, and now took more of a lead role in liaising with HLF on behalf of the Trust, seeking to establish a better working relationship with the local HLF officers.

Charitable Grants

From the beginning of the agreement to carry out a full restoration of the house that led to the appointment of a Preservation Trust, it became clear that MHPT could not rely solely upon the National Heritage Memorial Fund grant to fund the whole operation. We would need to seek other funds. This was a new development because when the application had first been made to the NHMF, the grant they promised would have covered the whole project including the provision of a Ministry Centre. If the work could have been started at that time, or shortly after, a lot of money could have been saved.

The major task of the fund-raising committee set up by the trustees and chaired by Sam Whitbread, as well as funding all the new finds, was now also to meet the increasing shortfall between the rising cost of the existing restoration and the fixed grant that was coming through HLF. The finance committee set to work straight away drawing on a number of different contacts. They recognised the advantages of the partnership between the Christian Ministries and the Preservation Trust that lay at the heart of this restoration project which enabled them to seek grants from both heritage and Christian charitable trusts even though building grants were outside the remit of many of the latter.

These were now being sought both in Britain and overseas – the non-British trusts being sought mainly in the USA.

Independent Advisory Reports

The application to the World Monument Fund, resulted in a necessary viability assessment before they would issue their grant. Their report for MHPT some years later when this was still dragging on, dated February 2003, put into words a significant reservation on the small size of the house and the limited facilities available. The report said that the house would only be viable if operated with the support of the Ministries and their volunteers, as had been originally envisaged. This later became known as the 'Martin Drury Report', but sadly, even then it was never fully accepted or understood by MHPT.

As mentioned, when Simon had been seconded from CCM to work with MHPT as Park Ministries, it was not long before he had been asked to take the minutes for MHPT and became their Company Secretary, ostensibly so that he would know what was expected of the trading arm, but without, unfortunately, any chance to share in the planning. Nevertheless, he was able to initiate several other independent Advisory Reports on the viability of the ideas being posited by the Board or the Trust. More about all these projects and reports will be outlined in the next volume as they became more important.

Procrastination

In 1999, as reported above, the problems in the delays in the administration of the NHMF grant had also created problems in cash flow and in the payments to contractors. Over prolonged periods there were constant delays in receiving payment from HLF for the draw-down of the grant, despite the issue of architect's certificates certifying that the work had been done. The delays could occur anywhere in the cumbersome HLF bureaucratic system, from the monitor, the case officer, heads of departments, the finance officers, or numerous others.

When complaints were made it was never possible to track down where the delay had occurred, as members of HLF staff always declared that they had passed the papers on to someone else. The delays were a constant source of embarrassment in relationships with contractors who had to meet their wages bills and to pay subcontractors as well as pay the accounts accrued for materials and overheads.

The Business Plan

It was vitally important to everyone that we had a viable Business Plan for the eventual running of the estate, and this became a further source of difficulty that lasted throughout the seven years of problems with HLF. Once again Simon, who had been delegated to carry the lead between HLF and MHPT was called upon to put this together with constant reference to others. This had to be produced and approved before the grant contract was even issued – a process that took many months and went through numerous revisions.

The Business Plan had to show how the House would be used following the completion of the restoration although at that time, in 1997, none of us knew that it was going to be a long time before the House would be anything like fully operational and that its use then would inevitably be different from that originally envisaged.

Each time more historic discoveries were made that required adjustments to the architect's plans, this not only increased costs, but also reduced the number of bedrooms available which consequently reduced the viability of the House as a Ministry/Conference Centre: this in its turn affected the changing Business Plan. There were also many ongoing discussions among the Ministries about the Business Plan each time it was revised (and we lost count of the revisions over the years!) and then it had to go through HLF's long-drawn-out critical scrutiny and approval process with interminable delays.

The impact of all these delays upon the restoration work was harsh and caused severe financial strains and difficulties for many – for the Preservation Trust, for the restoration programme, for the contractors and for their subcontractors.

Ironically, in spite of the constant delays, Simon and Jenny found ways of keeping the morale high among the public and volunteers with positive activities using the ancillary buildings and space to the best of their ability, so they did not feel deprived of what they had never had!

Stressful Negotiations

Eventually Andrew Ingrey-Senn, by the end of 1999, after two years in the role, found the strain of dealing with the HLF too much and resigned as Chairman of MHPT saying that if he had been dealing with people like this in his business he would have walked away long ago, although he stayed with Harvest Vision as a Trustee for a further ten years.

He was succeeded as Chairman by Henry Clark, a surveyor who had recently left working for the Crown Estates to run his own business. He had considerable experience of working with charities as well as experience in the business world. He made it clear from the beginning that he would only act as Chairman on an interim basis and after a short period in office, being no more successful in dealing with HLF than Andrew Ingrey-Senn, he resigned and Chris Izzard, who had not long been a Trustee, became the new Chairman of MHPT.

New Chairman

As the fourth Chairman of MHPT, Chris Izzard, took responsibility in 1999, just over two years since the Trust was formed. He also was a businessman of considerable experience and came in with his eyes open and aware of the difficulties. Chris was the chairman of an engineering group and brought a wealth of negotiating skill and patience into relationships with HLF. He too encountered the same problems and inconsistencies and delays that had wearied his predecessors, as the following note from one of his reports to his fellow trustees illustrates –

MHPT Chairman's Update, April 2000:

HLF appear to adopt a continuing aggressive stance, which more often than not borders on the critical without being aware of their own shortcomings and contributions to our current situation. Nothing will be achieved by adopting a similar response. We remain courteous and patient and await their response to our latest submission which they have told me will probably not be until after Easter. (Since dictating these notes H... M...[the current case officer] now says END of MAY – because it all has to go back to the NHMF Trustees – that does not look promising!!) Part of the concern is because we have removed considerable works etc from the original grant programme – they also regard the lift as significant, and I feel they need to be convinced about our ability to raise more money!

Desire for Control

Although the works referred to in this note were removed from the grant programme funded by HLF, they were not taken out of the project. They were simply funded by us from other sources, leaving more funding for the increased costs on the other agreed items. This applied to such as the specific grant that was obtained for the lift mentioned above, one from the Getty Foundation and others. But HLF took no account of this – as far as they were concerned, we had deleted some of the agreed works, so we were reneging on our agreement! Other grants were received dedicated to particular rooms, or to external features such as the verandas, or newly discovered internal features such as the 'oculus'. But HLF did not find it easy to cope with this concept. They also resented being just one contributor in a complex restoration project. They were not team players; they wanted to be in complete control of everything.

HLF were, of course, accountable for public money and would never take our assurances, verbal or written, that specific parts of the work would be funded from other sources. Everything not only had to be proved, but they would wait until we either had the money in the bank, or contracts were signed with other grant-making bodies, and they were given documentary proof. Only then would they accept changes to the original agreement with them and agree to allow work to continue. They worked from the premise that no one was to be trusted. The frustration caused by these delays is almost impossible to describe and we were, in consequence, constantly apologising to our professional team, and to contractors and subcontractors, one of whom went bankrupt waiting for payments from clients, to which we no doubt contributed.

HLF also insisted on major publicity being given to their grant and it being given priority on the notices on the site and grounds and in all reports of the progress of the work. They did not recognise that they were now only one of the grant-making bodies contributing to the restoration. They wanted to be the most prominent, and even the *only one acknowledged* – although their grant amounted to less than half the final total of the restoration.

Virtual Completion – at last!

It was not until the final stages of the internal works contract, described as 'virtual completion', drew near in 2004, that relationships really eased. By this time, a new monitor had been appointed who at last took a keen interest in the project and had a sympathetic understanding of the complex issues that were involved. He worked well with our professional team and did his best to facilitate a smooth path through the hostile HLF bureaucracy. No doubt this was made easier as we could no longer be dismissed as a group of idealistic Christians lacking in professional competence, but we had demonstrated beyond challenge that we had the ability to carry the project through to completion against all their fears (or negative expectations) to the contrary.

From London to Cambridge

It was with a tremendous sense of relief that the final payment was received from HLF and we no longer had to submit to the vagaries of the London office. The situation was helped as by this time, probably as the new venture of HLF was settling into a better *modus operandi*, responsibility had been devolved from central London to a regional office more locally and we were now dealing with the new one in Cambridge where a much more sympathetic atmosphere reigned, and staff appeared actually interested in the project. They even went so far as to say that sympathetic consideration would be given to a further application for assistance in the restoration of the grounds. But that would be a new phase in the life of Moggerhanger Park and if we decided to take that route, we now had more experience of what to expect!

But we are jumping ahead. This is a truncated description of all the complicated steps that Harvest Vision had to take, once they were granted that first major grant awarded in 1995 in order to get the work it was expected to cover, even started. It would be nine years later, in 2004 before we reached that stage, but what about the original group of Ministries who had had a vision and were just waiting to bring the building into use - which was their original purpose when the building was purchased?

Was the vision now changing too much? So much more went on during this lengthy period behind the scenes by those who were not prepared to wait just doing nothing while Harvest Vision and Moggerhanger House Preservation Trust fought their battles. Just as the community got involved where they could, many of these activities would, in spite of the delays, actually forward the work. We will now look at what had happened to the three main Ministries in the remaining years of the 20th century, and as the new millennium dawned.

Chapter Nine
THE MINISTRIES –
CONSOLIDATION AND CHANGE

In this chapter we look at the closing years of the 20ᵗʰ Century and the effect that the changes and delays in the restoration plans at Moggerhanger had on the Ministries. Conversely, unforeseen changes took place in the Ministries which, although unwanted and unexpected at the time, in the end brought fresh opportunities for cooperation and expansion.

Work on the restoration of the Main House may have hit problems and have been developing very slowly, but this did not hold back the plans of the Ministries. It was just that these other matters came to the fore and meant that changes were taking place there too.

CCM Main Ministry Moves in 1999

The Centre for Contemporary Ministry (CCM) had always had a representation at Moggerhanger although its main educational ministry was still being carried out at Bawtry Hall. We were in a Catch-22 situation waiting for accommodation to be ready for residential courses as well as the World Mission Study Centre, before the move could be made effectively. Its Trustees had been meeting at Moggerhanger whenever they met, but they were now in a similar position to the BCGA – having a token presence, and just an organisational headquarters there, while their main ministry activities were being carried out elsewhere: the major difference being that they did intend moving the whole of their well defined educational Ministry to the new premises at the right time.

CCM Trustees in their fairly dormant Headquarters at Moggerhanger, had therefore gladly accepted the proposal to form a department to run Moggerhanger Park in 1997 to be prepared for the great move. This final move of CCM courses and resources was now confirmed for 1999 as Lyn Wortley, our efficient Administrator at Bawtry Hall would have completed her training for ministry then. Although accommodation was not yet ready at Moggerhanger, the move from Bawtry Hall eventually took place just before she was ordained and inducted into the C of E in Greasbrough in South Yorkshire.

Now, at last, the three founding Ministries were to be together in one place for the first time – but not yet with the freedom to use the buildings in the way they had originally intended. The wider activities in which they were each involved had grown in importance although each of these was seen as a positive indicator that could also raise greater opportunities for the House itself to become more widely known and indirectly to have a share in being able to influence the nation. But the delays in the restoration were not permitting them to progress very easily – and even more changes were needed.

Cliff and Monica's Change of Emphasis

The travel problems that Cliff and Monica had experienced were an important factor behind the original purchase of Moggerhanger Park. These had been partially solved when they moved their homes into the area, but travel was still important as their national and international ministries expanded. London remained important and essential, but less than an hour away by train and for International travel they had substituted Luton and Stanstead for Gatwick and Heathrow!!

There had also been much planning for the future, particularly for the coordination and expansion of the Ministries now on-site – and this included Cliff and Monica's continuing role into the future and ultimately their own succession planning.

Monica had been leading the BCGA since the 1980 National Congress and Cliff had launched PWM out of the Video Nasties Parliamentary work in 1983 and it had expanded rapidly from 1985 with *Prophecy Today* and the 1986 Carmel / Jerusalem Gatherings. Once PWM was settled, and well before 1999 when succession steps began to be taken, both Cliff and Monica were expecting to hand the leadership of two of these main founding ministries over to others so that they could concentrate on CCM and any ministry at the house.

By June 2000, both Cliff and Monica had effectively completed the handing over of their leadership of their respective ministries PWM and BCGA. They were now operating much more in the background and at a different level. They wanted to concentrate on CCM and the projects now being coordinated by C&M Ministries outside Moggerhanger. CCM now had a responsibility for all the ministry at the Park which inevitably affected the in-service courses for clergy they were expecting to run through CCM. Unfortunately, neither PWM nor BCGA survived under their changed leadership – for different reasons which will be told in their own histories elsewhere.

Lessons on Staffing and Volunteers Learned

The problems encountered by the Ministries as they each settled into their new offices provided insights helpful for the future. In the 1990s, long before the widespread use of the internet and the mobile phone, there had been quite a turnover of staff from both BCGA and PWM when they had first arrived and this took time to settle down. Not only was housing a problem in bringing people in from outside the area, but travel was too, as having access to a car was almost an essential to being involved. Jerome Mouat, who lived in Cheltenham, had become Managing Editor of *Prophecy Today* on a part-time basis for around a year. We have memories of the whole community looking forward to his visits with great expectations as he combined this PT role with that of reviewing new cars for a national motoring magazine – he would test drive a different (often exotic) car each time he made the journey!

Volunteers at all levels were also an extremely important part of the team and it became rapidly obvious that travel and accommodation would always be at the top of the list for them too. Mike Baker had initially brought his own tent with him to enable his involvement! The Gatehouses and Bungalow had been given priority for restoration and anyone with their own transport persevered with their links. Malcolm and Margaret Baker had been coordinating our booklet printing and newsletter mailings from their school printing department in Folkestone. They used to come and stay in what we dubbed the 'caravan village'[1] which served them and other volunteers well for a while but was never intended to be long-term. The internet was still in its infancy and for full personal involvement it was becoming essential for staff to have their own transport, live locally or be willing to make the move, with the responsibility for other family commitments playing a key role in any decisions made.

PWM Developments

For the first two years after their move, PWM had prioritised the activities of their two major ministry arms - *Prophecy Today* and PWM Team Ministries. The latter was focused and strengthened by the vision of David Forbes for setting up a Biblical and Hebraic Study Centre which would also start with and then include correspondence courses and it was expected that travelling would reduce as this teaching arm developed.

Mervyn and Mair Pike brought the distribution of *Prophecy Today* from Maldon in Essex to The Park as a more central venue,

---

1   At one time we had three 'permanent' caravans on-site, all donated by prayer partners and hard standing for any mobile ones joining them with their owners when possible.

and trained Alison Cross and Louise Cooper to take subscriptions and the bi-monthly distribution to shops and agents.

During *Prophecy today's* first few years at Moggerhanger, the Charity Commission had received complaints that some of the content of *Prophecy Today*, now the largest Christian Magazine in the UK, was Islamophobic. A great deal of time and expense was incurred in trying to discover what this meant and locate where it had occurred. Any pending complaints which might have become charges were dropped when the Charity Commission were unable to define what was meant by 'being Islamophobic' but it had alerted the *Prophecy Today* Editorial Board to the need to pay extra care and to be prepared for further major changes coming their way.

But the overall turn-over of top-level staff being experienced, also meant constant training and change – and this, alongside the inauguration of a number of new ventures, was sadly followed closely by David's untimely death, and gave a feeling of instability in the team. David had been diagnosed with terminal cancer soon after the office move and he was never able to settle at The Park as planned and when he died on Good Friday 1998, things had got even more difficult.

Finding a New Way Forward

The Revd John Fieldsend, a one-time 'kinder child' and now a messianic Jew, left CMJ in nearby St Albans and took over the leadership of the developing CHBC department for a while and it began to expand not only with teaching days at The Park but with correspondence courses and tours to Israel – and also into Europe to the places where Judaism had thrived, but also where the holocaust had been rampant. C&M Ministries was able to give backroom help with any Overseas Tours organisation, especially the Israel teaching tours and resources, as they had done for all overseas ministry in the past.

Both CCM and C&M Ministries took an on-going interest in the Parliamentary research and cooperated in supporting the continuing family research team temporarily based at Moggerhanger which had expanded considerably since the meeting with Jack Straw in 1997 and the public meeting in the Moses Room mid-1998. Its work was becoming more formally established as the Family Matters Institute (FMI) and would soon have its first full-time director Lady Adey.

In Summer 1998 David Hilsley joined the team as overall Administrator for PWM working with Ruth Addington who by this time was firmly established as its general secretary and was particularly helpful to Cliff.

Revd Dr Walter Riggans, became PWM Deputy Director in September 1998 as the Biblical and Hebraic work expanded. Amelia's daughter-in-law, Karen, was his well-qualified secretary. Unfortunately, an extra-marital relationship developed which could not be resolved and the PWM Trustees dismissed them both less than a year later, leading to a threatened industrial tribunal which was dropped at the last minute after 6 months of anxiety. There were now two broken families resulting in the loss of Amelia from the Gatehouse and her community leadership before the end of the century, as she had to care for her son and grandchildren, plus a broken ministry from which PWM never fully recovered.

Park Expansion Opportunities

Ironically, the more National Ministry projects taking place outside of Moggerhanger were flourishing and we will look at these in the next chapter.

There were, though, also signs of further good news, as there were Christian groups, hearing that offices had been created to accommodate ministry activities, who were making enquiries for space and the possibility of becoming part of the Moggerhanger Community that was growing.

Scripture Union caught the vision as they needed to move away from London. They wanted to link with other Christian ministries, which led us to explore briefly the possibility of other groups becoming part of a larger consortium based together and sharing resources – but lack of space for this expansion led nowhere. The Billy Graham Evangelistic Association wanted to hold a conference here as a precursor to creating a central office on the site – but even the facilities to hold this were not yet available.

Similarly, through our growing Hebraic links, we had approaches in 1998 from newer sections of CMJ hoping at first for a small, dedicated piece of land for a cemetery for the growing number of Messianic Jews in this country, as they were now being excluded from being buried in Jewish cemeteries. Although impractical it led to the possibility of a Discipleship House for Jewish People. Stuart Cohen moved into the village and gave great support to this growing Hebraic Studies department.

Links were built with local churches at both a clergy and a people level, which expanded when Peter Eyre, a Baptist minister from Guernsey had spent the summer of 1995 on a sabbatical with us. In 1998, he became minister of Biggleswade Baptist Church and his appointment there lasted some seven years building up more links with local churches.

During the latter part of 2000, PWM Trustees had come to recognise that if PWM were to survive and be truly effective in its own right in these new surroundings, they would need to spend time reorganising their Ministry and the Trustees were grateful to be able to consult and pray with the leaders of the other Ministries on-site who had already seen the need to meet together regularly.

United Park Ministries Support

Working together and supporting each other in bad times as well as good, was seen as essential, and a Joint Ministries

Leadership team (JML) had been formed with the advent of PWM. This group met regularly, both to solve practical problems, not just in the areas of ministry for which they were each responsible, but to find other ways of supporting and working together recognising that they needed each other.

CCM, with their confirmed additional role of coordinating the Ministries at Moggerhanger, had sent out an illustrated 4-page Spring Newsletter early in 1998 introducing Park Ministries which included confirming Gillian Orpin's role as their Pastoral Minister from April, complete with a Venn Diagram of the relationship between the Ministries. This Park Mailing would become a regular mailing of combined activities to go alongside the news of building and restoration work sent out in MHPT Mailings that were also standardised at that time. This mailing included all the Joint Open Days alongside all the other activities now being organised and coordinated by The Park operating arm of CCM which had now moved to a new coordinating level.

'Park Ministries' had sent out the first Christmas 1999/2000 Greetings and News from the combined ministries which went to everyone and embraced those on all of the then separate mailing lists which often overlapped.

Mike Baker's only recently discovered additional computer skills were a great blessing and a major unifying joint achievement. He developed and coordinated the various lists using an Access database format and brought together all the contacts in the growing number of ministries into one joint basic entity, but with each having separately controlled dedicated branches. The supporters of each would still continue to receive separate information but they were now linked together into the Moggerhanger Community which gave both a unity and an in-depth involvement at the same time.

We were also blessed by one of the more unusual Park volunteers in 1997/8: Kate Stanley, the teen-age daughter of an Anglican clergyman who we soon discovered was anorexic and wanted to stay in the UK for six months, as her father took up an appointment in Australia. She joined the community in the Gatehouse at that time under Amelia's care. We discovered that she had an amazing artistic gift, and she began to make excellent drawings of different scenes around the site. One of the Ice House, part of a whole series which were later used in many ways, was used for the Joint mailings from this time.

Under Pressure

The support mechanism was good but not everyone felt the benefit. All the tension being experienced at this time in PWM, one of the main ministries, inevitably put extra strain on the whole community and inadvertently also on the MHPT Trustees who were at the same time having their struggles with HLF funding.

Dorothy Richards, our first Executive Secretary[2] was far from well and had recently had a fire in her home. She felt she could not carry the extra burdens being placed on her, so she resigned at the end of 1999 from both Harvest Vision and MHPT at the same time as Andrew gave up the chairmanship with the stress caused him by the HLF negotiations. Others had to be encouraged to carry on what was seen by some as an unnecessary and unwelcome battle. Ruth Addington, as well as agreeing to do secretarial work for C and M Ministries, then also took on Dorothy's secretarial role with MHPT following which the trustees employed a Secretary from outside for a short period until Simon took over.

PWM Developments

While PWM's future was being discussed, the PWM Team and supporters immediately rallied round their trustees to carry

---

2 To record our appreciation of the tremendous role she had played since the very beginning, a tree was planted near the Main House, with a plaque alongside.

on those parts of the Ministry work which were in danger of being lost and Dr Clifford Denton, who had been out of the general run of PWM activity since he gave over his dormant charity Harvest Vision to be revitalised in the 80s, took on a greater role in PWM itself particularly for the 'One New Man' planned international events and tours for Jerusalem 2000 in Israel with Fred Wright taking over the planned Journal for the Centre for Biblical and Hebraic Studies and getting involved in the Pardes teaching days.

Dr Peter Carruthers, and John Smith helped with the production of *Prophecy Today* and Cliff was then able to join Monica in giving more time to CCM and the coordination needed at Moggerhanger, although their international ministry in the Far East and Africa was also expanding at this time. A 4-page Annual Report with extra pages extracted from the April 1999-March 2000 accounts was circulated to the PWM supporters to keep them in touch.

PWM and CCM Proposed Merger

In June 2001 the decision of both sets of Trustees was to combine the PWM ministry with CCM activities, close both down and take legal advice on forming a new charity in the name of CCM. Neither of their original Trust deeds, as written, would enable them to take on the much wider breadth of Christian Ministry that was now envisaged – it was also felt that the wider nature of PWM had completed its task.

Prophecy Today would then become an independent company rather than a charity but would still be closely associated as the mouthpiece for the Ministry at Moggerhanger. David Andrew was appointed to take this forward with John Robbins and Alison Cross, and Cliff acting in an advisory founder capacity.

The Parliamentary research work on the Family was being supported by CCM already and was well on its way to becoming the Family Matters Institute and CCM now became the central ministry at Moggerhanger developing projects and linking others and supporting each other.

Clifford Denton then felt his season of helping was coming to an end as opportunities were opening up for his own overseas work. Dave Hilsley's retirement plans to move to the Moggerhanger area did not materialise as both his mother and mother-in-law were living on the Essex coast and he moved house in that direction to support them. By June 2000 Lee & Rosie Armstrong had joined the Pardes team and then John Smith. Neither made much progress on the original plans and eventually David Hilsley came back in to oversee and develop Pardes from a distance.

Shorty into the new millennium, CCM had successfully taken over PWM's on-going activities and was covering them although the merger had not officially been completed. The BCGA activities and sub-groups were thriving around the country with their headquarters remaining at Moggerhanger for a few more years.

Park Ministries

CCM, as well as the educational and wider ministry of PWM, now had a department 'Park Ministries' overseeing all on-site activity – whether this was being instigated by the Ministries or from outside. Cliff and Monica had dropped back into a coordinating role but retained directorship of CCM which was now acting as the liaison for all the Ministries' activities with Harvest Vision and MHPT.

In spite of all the changes taking place at this time, the underlying ethos of building and serving the community (both the local and wider community) underpinned everything we sought to do. The Vision and Mission as agreed in 1997 were reaffirmed and developed:

The Vision for The Park is that it will be:

- A Centre for Christians of all denominations, where they can come for prayer, study, recreation and Christian companionship.

- A Centre known to non-Christians as a place of openness, faith and commitment, where they are encouraged to know the word of God, and where they can see the love of Christ being expressed through words, actions and lives.

The Mission of The Park is that it will be:

- A place where training courses covering all aspects of the Christian Faith are run in a professional yet unworldly way, such that all those who attend may grow in their discipleship.

- A place which churches and Christian organisations will seek to use as their first choice when planning conferences, retreats, or fellowship gatherings.

- A place which demonstrates to the world how the message of Christ is of relevance and significance to contemporary business and society.

- A place where prayer is the basis behind all activities.

- A place which acknowledges the different worship styles and traditions between all Christian denominations, yet recognises the value of our common faith and heritage.

- A place where all aspects of the work show a positive witness for Christ, such that the world may be touched by the people who visit there, and the events that take place there.

How this all actually worked out and fitted in with our national and international ministry as we went into a new century, we will read more about in the next chapter.

Chapter Ten
INFLUENCING THE NATION

This chapter starts the new millennium with a catch up on what has been happening on-site. We then turn away from both the restoration of the house and activities at Moggerhanger to take a brief look at Ministry action on a wider field. It describes work in Parliament and national affairs which it was hoped would continue to open up doors for the use of Moggerhanger House. Alongside this, the birth of new Ministries brought new vision and fresh opportunities for expansion.

With the start of a new millennium and the active founding ministries having been reduced now to just two, there was still no date when the house could be used for ministry or public meetings. Having handed responsibility for the restoration to other specially formed charities while we were waiting, these Ministries concentrated their activities outside Moggerhanger.

More Founding Ministry Changes at Moggerhanger

The BCGA was expanding around the country but still had its headquarters in Moggerhanger located there from the days even before it was officially owned by Harvest Vision. Following Sheila's illness, there had been staffing changes and with both Philip Walker initially assisting Monica and gradually taking over leadership and Richard Quennell as our Book Manager and a growing number of books and volunteers, they needed more desk and people space than the small office they had occupied all along, so they had by 2000 developed the recently vacated space in the upstairs of the Grooms House opposite, into a self-contained small suite of offices plus store room.

This whole eastern section of the Stable Courtyard buildings was scheduled for development in Stage 2 when the first floor would be adapted for further residential accommodation and the ground floor would cease to act as Visitor Reception and become the BCGA office although it was planned that the second large ground-floor room would continue to be used as an Exhibition area. When Stage 1 was completed, it was also planned that Visitor Reception would then take place in the Main House. The grant money had been promised and was just waiting to be used, BUT no date had yet been set for the start of Stage 1, never mind its completion and moving on to Stage 2. But we carried on planning for the future in hope.

Library Plans

The arrival of all the books from the Study Centre at Bawtry Hall, plus the books from the Church Growth Book Service coming down from Scotland at the start of 1998, had led to the need to continue having them available as a library for both the CCM Courses and for the House.

We knew that all the great houses of the past had had their own Libraries. Plans were considered for the most likely room for this in Moggerhanger, and the north facing Drawing Room on the ground floor was felt to be right, backed up by an extended library in the Garden Room to help on the courses – and that as we had so many specialist books, the Lending Library concept could also become a great asset.

The basic cataloguing of these books had already been carried out by both the BCGA and CCM and the books now occupied an increasing number of shelves in the large, dedicated Library at Bawtry Hall and when it was transferred with CCM's other resources to Moggerhanger this was immediately added to the Furnishing Committee's remit. A Library Team from among the Ministries rapidly developed which included several professional librarians including John Kingham from among our prayer partners who were prepared to give time to physically cataloguing all the books and it was agreed to purchase our own Dewey cataloguing system and 'ResourceMate' became a major computer tool serving us well for many years.

Each of the Ministries was adding their own resources and also providing specialist consultants willing to give first hand teaching and advice to visitors. It was agreed that both library and consultant facilities could be provided by the Ministries when the House was open. This was already being used to a minor degree and it was believed that it could expand considerably when accommodation became available – there was even talk of having special weeks when a well-known leader, writer or academic, would be in residence giving lectures and seminars which would attract others to stay.

One of the Library team, Alyson Hogarth, a Librarian in Middlesbrough Library, had alerted us to plans to close one of their branches in the North of England and when this happened in 2004, their shelving system, in tip-top condition, was collected and installed in the far end of the Garden Room where it served both the Ministries and community well for a number of years. The whole Library concept was now being used and developed much further.

Future of BCGA

Monica had led the British Church Growth Association since it was first envisaged at the National Congress on Evangelism in 1980 but Philip had now taken over the sole leadership on a paid basis (with a 'seed money' grant) so that Monica could give more time to CCM and Moggerhanger Park. Unfortunately, by mid-2003, when the grant ceased, it was struggling financially and the BCGA Council (the first of the founding ministries to be resident), agreed that the Association had finished its role in stimulating Church Growth in the UK, and that Philip should concentrate in a consultancy role on

Natural Church Development, renaming the work 'Healthy Church UK'. The BCGA closed down and a Thanksgiving Service was held in central London on 3rd October 2003. The BCGA had set in place autonomous networking groups with agreed leadership – the Small Church Network, the Church Planting Initiative and the European Church Growth Association which were all encouraged to continue independently. Philip ran the Healthy Church UK from home and continued supporting the Joint Ministries and became a Trustee of CCM in 2007.

Richard then took the books he felt were currently saleable from the large number of books in stock in this category, so that he could establish a private enterprise bookshop from home and carried on distributing books on request. The Church Growth Library, though, was considered to be an important unique asset and although Training Colleges were bidding to take this over, it was agreed that it would stay at Moggerhanger as part of the burgeoning Library there as a resource which might attract visitors. C&M Ministries gave a donation of £2,000 for it to remain at Moggerhanger.

Chapel Provision and Spiritual Preparations

From the beginning, there had never been any intention to have a church on-site. There were two churches in the village, and we saw the buildings, and the facilities at Moggerhanger, as being a major resource for ALL the churches round about, not just one which would inevitably have one or other denominational base to which it would be linked.

We were also well aware that when the Thornton family were in occupation, the Anglican Church in Blunham was the nearest church and was where the family were all buried. In the late 1700s and early 1800s, even though the family would attend this local church, all the great houses would also have had their own chapel – not just for the owners but increasingly becoming a place in the home for the household community. There were, however, no architectural plans found for a chapel at Moggerhanger. It was noted that St John's C of E was built in 1860 in the northern area of Moggerhanger by Elizabeth Dawkins in memory of her husband Revd Edward Dawkins who died within two years of purchasing the estate after the Thornton family had sold the house in 1850 so it did have some links with the House.

A cross denominational praying community had been involved from the beginning of our occupation at Moggerhanger and now that Gillian Orpin had linked with St John's and was preaching there regularly, she joined the community pastoral team to lead the mission outreach on-site, and a chapel became a unifying priority. Mrs Thornton's Boudoir between the two main bedrooms at the top of the stairs on the first floor was felt to be a natural and agreeable possibility as it was in a prime position but not large enough to be used as a bedroom.

Gatehouse Changes

Amelia's role as Gatehouse Hostess was now being fulfilled by Linda and Chris Brett who moved into the second Gatehouse at the start of 2000. Chris continued to self-support the two of them during their time of tenure and they quickly settled into the hosting role as well as taking over on-site security and wider community development on the estate.

Chris was tall and heavily built and he would regularly patrol the grounds in the evenings. He dealt firmly with a group of local teenage boys who were breaking the glass in an old greenhouse no longer in service. They pleaded that they were simply letting loose their energy in this way – but they did not argue with Chris, and he persuaded them to come back to engage in more creative work. He built a good relationship with the lads. Linda's Friday fry-up breakfasts for the workmen became extremely popular, known as 'Greasy Spoon Fridays'. They were providing a valuable link between the on-site community and the increasing numbers of contractors who were employed to restore the main house.

Other Opportunities

An open event *'Moggerhanger through the Ages'* was planned for 2004 and additional research was carried out on the evacuated school of 1914 and especially the more recent hospital days of ocupation. Many of our visitors remembered the latter – either visiting relatives in the hospital or having been here themselves. There was widespread recognition of a sense of peace that people experienced as they came on-site.

Interest was growing in Moggerhanger throughout the nation as the word spread around. Ways of bringing in extra funding were attempted but, following an approach from a film maker who paid a visit in 2002, whose main interest was in using its decrepit state and the outside decay for a Gothic tragedy, we drew the line at some! We welcomed other ventures, from Trade and Craft Fayres to the selling of superfluous or unwanted materials. The possibility of holding Auctions was explored - a successful *'Auction of Promises'* with the services of a professional Auctioneer was held in the Garden Room in 2004.

And on to the Newly Acquired Grounds

We already had a strong team of volunteers clearing and maintaining the grounds, but as the Walled Gardens and adjoining land and woods had recently been acquired, their cultivation and use were also now being carefully planned.

There was much natural beauty[1] and Snowdrop Walks and Bluebell Walks became very popular annual events but they required much preparation and planning. There were excellent viewing points around the estate and fresh signs of previous historic activities to be followed through.

We had learned how Humphry Repton's landscaping plans differed from those of Capability Brown, his illustrious

1 This included many spectacular trees such as the 200 year old Copper Beech on the Back Lawn, the Cedar used as an initial logo for the volunteers and a towering Redwood behind the Offices in the Stable block.

predecessor of a generation before, and, if we wanted to discover any guidelines either on how it was envisaged or on how it was actually put into use, we needed to locate Repton's Little Red Book of Moggerhanger House which he would have drawn up at the time.

It was well known that Humphry Repton was very community minded and believed in the civic responsibility of the numerous new landowners who had gained control of so much previously common land following the Enclosures Act of 1801. Repton was an ideas visionary who would produce before and after pictures and agree them and the subsequent plans with his clients – in this case members of the Thornton family. He would take account of their responsibility to the local people but would then leave the outworking and appointment of the workforce needed to the commissioning Family to carry out. It was known that the Thorntons had engaged him as their consultant on two occasions once in 1792 and then again in 1798. Having copies of those Little Red Books was to be of prime importance.

Work started on clearing the Walled Gardens and we were able to utilise supervised teams on probation, mainly boys and men recognisable by their yellow jackets, carrying out their community service. This developed into establishing our own Leadership Development Group with Ray Lewis, whose teams and programmes flourished for a while, and Youth Matters, a Bedford-based charity, with Doug McWilliams, helped especially in the Walled Gardens.

By this time John Drake, a local accredited landscape consultant, had been appointed as an MHPT Trustee and one of the first things he promoted in the Walled Gardens was a well-attended Sculpture Exhibition in September 2002.

Publicity for the House at the CRE[2]

BCGA, PWM and CCM had been among many Ministries and Christian organisations who had all appreciated the week-long opportunity to set up a stand and meet and share their ministries with others in Sandown Park for the Christian Resources Exhibition (CRE) held in May each year.

By May 2000 it was felt that the facilities at Moggerhanger Park were sufficiently developed to warrant booking a united stand in the name of Moggerhanger Park Ministries. It was felt that this would widen the publicity, as well as encourage visitors to use the facilities rapidly becoming available. Jenny organised the stand with the help of a rota of volunteers who drove to Epsom each day, stopping first at the Gatehouse to collect packed lunches for each of the volunteers taking part.

The CRE stand manned annually in Esher was used to publicise the facilities and events at Moggerhanger Park as well as for selling books and resources produced by the various Ministries. This continued for a number of years, with Monica and Cliff often being invited to speak at seminars and other events at the Exhibition and they also took part in a number of the CRE Regional events.

Researching the Thornton Roots

For a brief period, the three founding ministries had at last all been on one site at Moggerhanger but only while we were still waiting for residential accommodation to become available. In the meantime, CCM had taken over PWM's family research for Parliament and they also started studying the links between the Clapham Sect and the Thornton Family and their links with Moggerhanger House.

---

2 The CRE was another venture coming out of the NCE in 1980 and was the brainchild of Gospatric Home and figures more largely in the next volume.

In 2000, Rodney Curtis, one of our prayer partners, took this on as a research project and a leaflet was produced to join those which Dorothy Richards had already produced on John Soane and Humphry Repton. '*Rediscovering the Heritage of Moggerhanger House and the Ethos of the Clapham Sect*' was made available as a four-page leaflet to all visitors.

Rodney had produced enough material for a book as well as an exhibition which we were able to draw on in many other ways. He had built extensively on the exhibition we had made in 1996 for the Coutts Bank enterprise, which had also been on display in the Bank of England and then transferred (considerably expanded) to the Stable Courtyard. This Exhibition became the main attraction at the 'Ministries at Moggerhanger' Open Day in July 2003 where plans were also shared of developing a large library.

While Rodney was carrying out his research, Monica had also begun to research, and make contact with, the descendants of the Thornton Family in order to build up the family links and alert them to the vision and potential changes taking place. Many were not too far away so they came for the Ministries Open Day mentioned above – even a 'Descendants Weekend' event at Moggerhanger was organised for others so they could meet with each other, and more involvement was promised for the future.

Good News on the House!

In the midst of all the activity occupying the Ministries at this time, in 2001, we heard that at last, the work was going to start on the actual restoration of the House and we could begin to forward plan. Our original plans for a grand opening were being changed and updated all the time, and we began to work positively towards 2004 as the date when at least some sections would be open and in use although we realised that even our initial plans would not be fully completed at that time. We also were realistic in believing that the work would never actually be 'fully finished' – there would always be more to develop and upgrade – and then there would always also be continuing maintenance!

When the opportunity arose in 2001 to arrange for the incoming Archbishop of Canterbury, Rowan Williams to be present at the opening in 2004 and put the house officially on the map, we began to make fuller plans and confidently work towards that date.

Books and Resources

Both Rodney's and Monica's research had by this time highlighted the first of the 'Objectives' of the Clapham Sect – the 'Reformation of Manners'[3] or as Wilberforce often described it 'Making Goodness Fashionable'. They each picked up the emphasis that Henry Thornton, the great philanthropist, was making in the late 18th century when Moggerhanger House was being recast.

This was the time when Henry Thornton was introducing daily prayers into the great houses of the land. Monica had set about producing, in more modernised and relevant English, a commemorative limited edition of a sample week of these prayers (morning and evening) from his highly acclaimed 18th century *Family Prayers* publication so that it could be used in the bedrooms of Moggerhanger once the house was fully occupied. It was called *Thornton Family Prayers*.

Cliff was writing a much larger volume entitled *The Wilberforce Connection*, which also majored on Wilberforce's aim of changing the values in the nation – in addition to the Abolition of the Slave Trade. This was to trace the development of society in Wilberforce's day and look at the relevance of his

---

3   The second of Wilberforce's objectives, often better remembered, was 'the Abolition of the Slave Trade' which he did manage to achieve in his lifetime.

work for Moggerhanger today. In both eras there was a need for both society and church to change and he listed seven lessons which could be drawn from the 18th century Clapham Sect which could be part of a 21st century Clapham initiative based at Moggerhanger –

1 an emphasis on love, not fear

2 an emphasis on ethical values

3 integrity and perseverance

4 seeing the wider picture

5 building community

6 building relationships,

7 home and away.

These fitted in well with the plans for the future at Moggerhanger Park and we made plans to coincide the publishing of both these books with the opening of the House in 2004.

Clapham Connections Initiative

In the year 2000, we began to discuss openly the possibility of a **21st century Clapham Initiative** based at Moggerhanger and we began to circulate monthly news information sheets and 'Clapham Comments' papers linking prayer partners into a network of action. These linked people together for a number of years through a website which listed eight national objectives of 'Clapham Connections' and seven local objectives which related to activities at Moggerhanger House. Two papers on community transformation followed, *'Mobilising the Grassroots',* and *'Order out of Chaos'.*

Cliff's Parliamentary work gave him access to Members of both Houses of Parliament and he established friendships with many of those who were active Christians. The interest in Wilberforce was growing at that time, as we were approaching the 200ᵗʰ anniversary of the 'Abolition of the Slave Trade' in 2007.

This led to the desire among Mps to be part of a similar group seeking to establish Christian values in society today, and to reverse the strong moves toward secularisation that were threatening the Judaeo-Christian foundations of the nation. Alistair Burt, who was Chairman of 'Christians in Parliament' in the early 2000s was a local Bedford MP with connections to Moggerhanger Park. He chaired a number of meetings for Christian Workplace Associations that led to the formation of the *Christian Workplace Forum* based at Moggerhanger for a number of years and also brought together the group that led to the formation of *Transform UK*.

Christian Workplace Forum

CWF began this new ministry by looking at what was already happening around the country in the world of work; noting the increasing number of Christian groups that were being formed in a workplace environment – usually breakfast or lunch-time groups.

Research with representatives of the many paragroups representing the professions was reported at a meeting in the House of Commons by the Parliamentary Christian Fellowship in 2003. This had a common goal of seeking greater understanding of the application of Christian ethics in the workplace and discovering how Christians could be more effective in bringing their faith into all areas of the economy.

It was at this stage in 2003, that Ros Turner joined the staff of CCM to assist in the development of the *Christian Workplace Forum*. This forum was based at Moggerhanger for a number of years working on strategies for change that would bring Christian principles and biblical values into the workplace.

Two specific ventures underwriting this work were seeking to ensure that Christians were able to share their faith with others in the workplace and looking for opportunities of making biblical values influential in boardroom policy decisions. 'Christians in the Audit Commission' were particularly successful in the second of these, paving the way for influencing at a board level when their representative was offered a place on the Board. They were given an opportunity to share Kingdom principles with a 'Thought for the Day' based on biblical principles being circulated centrally.

Transform-UK

The concept was also picked up nationally with *Transform UK* drawing together many larger action groups such as the still infant Christian Concern, Barnabas Fund, and the Bible Society, alongside uniting various Christian Professional Associations – their ethos was not that of a new organisation with a membership that people joined. It was rather like the many people who had followed the Clapham Group, it was to be a *movement* not an organisation and a series of papers called 'Clapham Connections' followed.

It was intended to encourage cooperation, sharing of information and resources, thus adding value and direction to work that was already in progress. Its major aim was establishing links with a wide range of people involved in activities that would influence the values of the nation and thereby initiate creative social change. One of their earliest campaigns was to organise Hustings around the country for the 2001 General Election and then to join together to present a programme and presentation on a national Tour of the major cities in 2003. Rowan Williams had readily endorsed *Transform-UK* which led to leaders of other churches also taking an interest.

Parliamentary Work

But our parliamentary work had been building on even deeper roots. In February 1996 in the early days of settling in at Moggerhanger, Cliff's earlier research work on Video Violence and Children from 1983 (which had provided the initial support base in the formation of PWM) had been followed by a reinvigorated cross-party 'Lords and Commons Family and Child Protection Group'. This group had appointed an Academic Working Party to carry out a year-long research programme on the severly topical extent of Family Breakdown which led to the *Family Matters* Report in 1998 mentioned earlier.

This research element continued from that time, and Moggerhanger Park had become the research base for the Parliamentary research group first under PWM's banner and then under that of CCM. In 2000 the foundation was laid for the formation of the 'Family Matters Institute' that later became a major sector in the group of Ministries based at Moggerhanger Park. During this period, they had produced more original research projects including two in the year 2000: '*Sex Under Sixteen*' and '*The Cost of Family Breakdown*'. The latter was recognised as a standard work in Parliament and was often consulted in the Parliament's library and quoted in debates by Members in both Houses of Parliament and is still referred to today.

To follow up these reports and to carry out further research at the request of the Lords and Commons Group, Cliff and Jenny now started to develop a separate team of volunteers from among the Community at Moggerhanger to develop some related parenting resources. They had organised a Resources Day in October 1998 with another event at Brickhill Baptist Church Bedford. Jenny continued to support the Family Matters work as part of CCM, helping to plan and establish FMI as a separate organisation until the Family Matters Institute became a registered charity and Lady Adey was appointed as FMI's first director in July 2000.

The Charity was launched with much publicity and a demonstration of the 'Flat Pack Parent' at the local branch of IKEA. Over the next 20 years it would exercise an influential national ministry with various projects including '*Dad Talk*' which had more than one million men registered on its database.

All these connections with Members of Parliament and the work done at Moggerhanger Park in connection with the publication of reports presented to MPs were seen as preparing the way for Moggerhanger Park to play an important role in the life of the nation once the restoration of the buildings had been completed.

Doors were opening for MPs and other groups to use the venue for retreats, but once again the vision ran ahead of the reality – the seemingly endless restoration of the buildings.

'Slavery' advance notice

Our interest in the connections with the Clapham Sect was opportune, as national plans were being drawn up for the commemoration of the 200th anniversary of the abolition of the slave trade to take place in 2007. There were many events linked to this anniversary, including the publication of the film 'Amazing Grace' by Walden Media, about the life and work of William Wilberforce that drew public attention to Wilberforce and the group of MPs that he led. Preparations for the commemorations, which included a service in Westminster Abbey, had begun several years earlier than 2007 with the setting up of a national committee of which Cliff and Monica were both serving members.

International Links

Our international travel had increased rather than diminished, and in the new millennium we had accepted an invitation to attend the Presidents Prayer Breakfast in Washington DC. We travelled out as part of a party from the UK, and we got to know Alistair Burt MP and his wife Eve personally. Although in the 1970s and 1980s we had made several exchanges in the summer months with ministers from churches in the Northern States this had been the only time we had visited the US in Winter or ventured into any of the Southern States. We made several other visits in the USA at this time which we hoped could reap benefits for Moggerhanger Park in the future.

Monica had also been making regular visits to different parts of Europe as the European Church Growth Association developed and her colleagues overseas were looking forward to the chance of having one or other of their 'Think Tanks' or conferences at Moggerhanger as soon as it became available. In 2003 the main ECGA international 3-day Conference was held in the Lake District, as Moggerhanger House was still not available.

Serious civil unrest prevented us going to Nigeria to link up with church and state early in 2000, to celebrate the election of the first Christian President. Dr Mary Lar, who became Ambassador to the Netherlands had written her book *Ambassador for Christ* at the Gatehouse in 1997 and our visit (by special invitation) later that year coincided with Bill Clinton's official visit from the USA, so we dined with two Presidents and built up many friendships which boded well for further international links with Moggerhanger.

A visit to the Far East in 2001 had not only supported a Missionary Training College in Indonesia but also established links with the Cathedral in Singapore. They then gave practical support when the 'Ambon Massacres' were taking place. These international links had much potential for the future. As too did the various teaching tours we took from the UK to Israel and the Mediterranean countries.

Monica had been invited to teach the practical element of Church Growth by Dr William Wagner at the Golden Gate Baptist Seminary in California in Spring 2003. This visit at this specific time enabled us to visit not only the Soane Museum in San Francisco, but also the Getty Foundation in LA who had given a grant to Moggerhanger House. Our US visit was not just one-way traffic. Members of the US Soane Society came to the UK in 2001 – eager to see the Moggerhanger House and help.

These were useful links we had then built upon and made a 43 slide powerpoint presentation which we were able to share and raise interest in arranging a further visit to the UK for them to see the House. We spent a day at the Getty Museum, which enabled us to report on the spending of their gift to the House. The new millennium gave us great hope for the future – and we wanted to ensure that we were ready for all the good times ahead.

Re-visiting the Vision

At a combined meeting of all the Ministries, the community, Harvest Vision and MHPT Trustees in June 2003, the basic Vision and Mission were confirmed as remaining the same as they had been in 1997 and which we printed at the end of the last chapter.

At this time, we were seeing more clearly the various avenues opening up and wanted to preserve them. The following nine points were agreed and used as a yardstick to measure future change:

Here is the Vision statement as elaborated in 2003, over the page:

Moggerhanger Park is –

1 A base for various ministries

We will continue to offer office space for all the on-site Ministries who want it (and hopefully, better quality services such as heating etc, as well!)

2 A resource for the on-site Ministries

We will provide any conference, residential and catering required to enable on-site Ministries to run courses, hold meetings, etc

3 A resource for Christians of all denominations

We already provide day conference facilities for local churches and other groups, as well as limited accommodation – this should increase as our full facilities become available.

4 A resource for the local community

We have already worked hard to ensure the local community sees us as an asset rather than a threat. Events such as the Family Open Day (where the local school performs) and the Bonfire Night Party help with this.

We are also beginning to develop educational links with the school, links with St Johns, and other links which can be seen as an asset to the village.

Additionally, resources such as the Tea Rooms and Garden Room will hopefully be seen as an asset.

5 A resource for wider society

This area became more significant as more was discovered about the heritage of the estate. Originally it was envisaged that we may attract a few non-Christians to the events and courses we were planning to run. However, it became evident that we would be attracting large numbers of non-Christians to our own events as well as just to view the House itself.

This was seen as an opportunity for witness: a means of fulfilling one of our original objectives – *'A Centre known to non-Christians as a place of openness, faith, and commitment, where they are encouraged to know the word of God, and where they can see the love of Christ being expressed through words, actions, and lives'.*

6 A place of refuge

We were already able to provide residential accommodation for private retreats and are becoming known as a place of peace and re-creation. We aimed to continue offering this both in the Gatehouse and in the Main House when it is open. Linda and Chris Brett were effectively – and naturally – taking on the role of providing support and ministry to those in need of refuge (a task that they were very well gifted to do).

7 A place of study

An important part of the resources we hope to have available in the House are the Library and Study Centre. These should provide facilities both for Christians and those wishing to study the architectural and historical aspects of the estate. We aim to be able to cater for private study as well as for organised courses for both Christians and non-Christians.

8 A place of teaching

Whilst Moggerhanger Park will not in the most part organise any teaching itself, it is hoped that this aim will be achieved through the facilitation of events run by the various on-site Ministries.

9 A place of prayer

Prayer has always been an important part of the life of the community of believers who founded Moggerhanger Park. It plays an essential role in giving guidance to the Trustees in making the decision that Moggerhanger Park was the place to which God had led us. Prayer continues to be an essential part in the life of the growing community in the early years of the settlement.

Chapter Eleven
PLANNING THE GRAND OPENING – ON OR OFF?

For the second time, we start planning for the opening of the house as the restoration appears now to be nearing completion. It was anticipated that the Main House would be ready for Ministry use in 2004 – after ten years of restoration. Coordinated joint plans are going well and then dry rot is discovered. The Ministries come to the rescue and the Grand Opening is transformed into a celebration of the Spiritual Heritage of Moggerhanger Park.

By 2002, Bowmans, who were now the main contractors carrying out the internal restoration work, had been able to give us a completion date of February 2004. So hopes were high that 2004 would indeed be the year of the fulfilment of our hopes and dreams; the restoration, or at least this initial stage, would be completed – and we would be able to celebrate the Grand Opening to the public. It may be ten years later than originally planned, but there was now much more for which to praise God – and we would be able, at last, to organise our in-service training programme for church leaders in our own Ministry Centre with CCM returning to its original purpose.

Bowmans did have an early setback with the discovery of an ancient well in the basement which caused problems, but they had assured us that they were still on target to complete the work by the end of May 2004. This would still leave us time before the Opening Day we were now planning to hold in early Autumn 2004.

Interested Parties

This phase of the building restoration work on the Grade 1 listed property had actually taken three years from 1998 to 2001 just to prepare plans and get the necessary agreement of all the interested parties. These were English Heritage, the Georgian Group, the Fine Arts Commission, the Bedfordshire County Conservation Officer, the Mid-Beds District Council Planning Committee, the Fire Officer, Health and Safety, (plus numerous others like the 'Beds Bats Society') and of course HLF and the trustees of the National Heritage Memorial Fund, plus the MHPT trustees, our architects, surveyors, and other members of the professional team, and last, but probably not least, the Ministry leaders who at this stage were still being consulted. It was indeed a complex operation!

Consultation Process

Before any agreements on any of these proposed house restoration plans could be obtained, this lengthy consultation-process had had to take place with many individuals and organisations. The most important sources of information on historic work were in the Sir John Soane Museum in London whose staff freely made available the plans and documents in their possession which related to Soane's work at Moggerhanger. Peter Inskip, our historical architect, took the lead in this work and in carrying out the detailed research required, room by room, throughout the House. This included paint and wallpaper analysis as well as details of the plaster work in each room so that a genuine restoration could be undertaken.

The actual building work had then eventually begun in August 2001 and had been scheduled to last two-and-a-half-years.

Park Ministries becomes MPL

By 2003, as we felt that the restoration work was nearing completion, alongside the work involved in co-ordinating all the proposed activities on-site and finalising plans for moving into, and use of, the Main House, it was also becoming obvious that CCM could no longer carry all this, as well as picking up and developing its original Ministry of running in-service training courses for those in Christian leadership. It became apparent that a dedicated organisation was needed – and Moggerhanger Park Ltd (MPL) was therefore established, with Jenny and Simon moving from CCM to run this new organisation. They now took on the main responsibility for co-ordinating all activities on the estate, working towards full opening of the House to the public as well as providing office and meeting facilities for the Ministries.

As the restoration progressed, we capitalised on the delays in order to publicise the house. We offered pre-arranged tours around the house and grounds, with the building contractors ensuring safe access. Throughout the Autumn and Winter of 2003/4 Simon and Jenny were invited to speak at numerous local history societies, WIs, and Rotary Clubs. These groups had started to book private tours of the house to see what was happening. We also started to run public tours twice daily each weekend throughout the summer.[1]

Since the Main House was still, in the main, largely a building site, the Garden Room (the last remaining prefabricated hospital ward on the back lawn) became the main hub of operations. Simon and Jenny were joined by catering manager, Jim Fitzgerald, who established a very popular Tea Rooms in the Garden Room, and tours of the House and grounds were run from there as well. The route of the tours varied according to which areas of the house were accessible at any given time – and it was quite a challenge to ensure that visitors were able to

1 Staff and volunteers were easily identifiable by their matching uniform and badges, which helped create a community spirit.

see as much of the house as possible whilst ensuring their safety and dodging the builders.

Our ever-expanding annual programme of events led to more and more visitors enjoying events such as Snowdrop Walks; Bluebell Walks; Craft Fairs; Family Fun Days and Firework Displays, as well as Regular Tours of the House.

Benefits

Moggerhanger Park was now becoming known as a lovely place to visit, and the tourism element of the work was proving highly successful. Many local people, in addition, remembered personally its days as a hospital and were eager to visit it now. The Visitors' Book for this period was crammed full of expansive praise both for the food and for the staff.

There was one good financial problem which arose – the tips for the staff and volunteers serving at the tables grew! A united decision was made that there should be a common purse and that all the volunteers and staff – on the grounds and behind the scenes should benefit. Rather than dividing this up between individuals, this was used for combined events, special meals, and theatre visits to London. These were opened to others who paid their way to be part of the community and we ourselves joined them for an evening coach outing to see Wilkie Collins 'The Woman in White' in the West End – their choice – probably because they had memories of Moggerhanger as it once had been!!

In addition, in their comments, many visitors spoke of the atmosphere being experienced as soon as they entered the estate, and it was this kind of commendation that really pleased us. It brought visitors from a wide area to Moggerhanger Park.

Further Public Interest in the Restoration

During this time, public interest in the work at Moggerhanger had been growing steadily over the prolonged period of the restoration. From time to time, both BBC and ITV sent film crews to record progress which was broadcast on regional TV. This helped enormously in bringing the house to the attention of the public in the region. But, by far, the best advocacy for the house was the word of mouth commendations from those who came and dined in the Tea Rooms when they also began to open up in the Main House, where a range of delicious food was already now on offer – courtesy of Jim FitzGerald who so believed in the project, and the way it was being worked out, that he had given his professional services at cost to Moggerhanger Park Ltd or Park Ministries as it was now better known.

Then, on the Sunday before National Heritage Weekend in September 2003, *The Observer* devoted a four-page colour supplement in its magazine to a report on the restoration work in Moggerhanger House. It had photos of the work on the ceiling of the entrance hall and the newly reconstructed oculus on the first floor. This was all free publicity, and it had the effect of bringing more than 2,000 people to view the House on that one Saturday afternoon!

Adapting Plans for Expansion

During the week following the publication of this Sunday newspaper, urgent discussions took place directly between the MHPT trustees, MPL and the Ministry leaders. This was the first time that any serious detailed discussion had taken place between those responsible for the physical work of the restoration and the Moggerhanger praying community who had been responsible for the original acquisition of the estate on actual specific event opertion. Volunteers were desperately needed to cope with the expected influx of visitors the following weekend – and they responded. The outline of the intended future use of the buildings, as agreed in the last chapter, was agreed by all.

This was only one month before the Ministries' own 'Open Day' on 18th October 2003 which this year was themed around the 'Thornton Family', and their links with William Wilberforce, the Abolition of Slavery, and the Clapham Sect with the movement of social reform that they had led in Georgian England. Ministry supporters were used to coming to Open Days at Moggerhanger, but this was the biggest event we had so far organised. The Ministry leaders also appealed for volunteers and there was a magnificent response. Everyone wanted to ensure that a good impression was being given to the public, and they saw the opportunity for using the buildings to make the best witness so far to their Christian faith.

The Ministry staff and volunteers in their respective communities helped to get the building into 'visitable' order each Friday evening once the building construction team had left at the end of the day. Jenny and Simon and their team provided and trained volunteers to cover a variety of jobs from car marshalling and car park attendants, to preparing and serving refreshments coordinated and prepared by Jim, our now fully involved chef, in various places; from room guides to a general organisational 'welcome team'. Those with no specific job were encouraged to mingle with the crowds to keep their spirits up and to share the story of the restoration with individuals.

Large Numbers of Visitors

On the Heritage Open Day itself in September 2003 the crowd waiting to enter the house was so great that the queues stretched back from the front door, some four or five deep for about a hundred yards. There were similar queues for refreshments, especially for the provision of burgers and chips! Our fledgling refreshment team was stretched beyond measure, but somehow they managed to feed everyone.

Great interest was shown by the visitors in the new ceiling under construction in the entrance hall featured in *The Observer,* and in the recently discovered oculus on the first floor. The volunteer guides who had been given a crash course in Soane's plans for these two architectural features gave their explanations throughout the day and did their best to answer as many of the technical questions as possible.

This huge public interest in the restoration of the house was a great encouragement to the whole Moggerhanger family as we all saw this as part of God's strategy in giving us such an historic House. It was notable that in addition to interest in the architecture, most people asked two questions – *"Who used to live here?"* and *"What are you doing with it now?"* This gave us an ideal opportunity for sharing our faith, through recounting the history of the Thornton and Wilberforce families, and how they put their Christian faith into action, not only in the abolition of slavery, but also in tackling some of the social and industrial issues and the injustices and inequalities in late 18th century and early 19th century Britain – and the evidence of this was apparent in their home and activities.

Opportunities for the Gospel

The large number of visitors also gave volunteers an opportunity of speaking about the work of the Ministries at Moggerhanger Park today where we were engaged in seeking to apply Christian principles to the social issues of the day through our Parliamentary work and other practical activities. All the volunteers were excited at the end of the day, recounting many interesting conversations with members of the public where they had had opportunities to talk about their ministry work and of sharing their faith.

Visitors were particularly interested in the connection of the house with William Wilberforce and the Clapham Group, who were, of course, best known for their contribution to the abolition of slavery. But our volunteer guides had all been instructed also to emphasise the other work of the Clapham Group and their interest in social reform at home such as the banning of sending small boys up the chimneys as sweeps from which they often received life-changing wounds and burns.

The guides were also keen to tell the public about the only book that Wilberforce himself wrote with its lengthy title, *A Practical View of The Religious System of Professed Christians in the Higher and Middle Classes in this Country Contrasted with Real Christianity.* It was hardly necessary to describe the content of this book – which was all there in the title! It gave the guides a great opportunity to speak about their own faith in the context of the situation in Britain today. They were all keen to share their experiences with the other volunteers at the end of the day when there was great rejoicing and a general sense of encouragement that, at last, we were nearing the point of seeing the Moggerhanger Ministry Centre at work. The Tensions and hard work had all been worthwhile.

Marketing Strategy

Showing to the public the half-finished House was, in fact, a great unplanned marketing strategy! Everyone was saying that they would come back to see it the following year when the work was expected to be completed. In the event, a year passed, and the House was once again opened for public tours through the summer of 2004, although, once again tours were operated from the Garden Room as the house was still far from being finished or open on a more regular timetable. Once again large numbers came, especially on the Heritage Weekend in September when some 3,000 visitors went on booked conducted tours.

As in the previous year, many more people declared that they would come yet again the following year to see what they hoped would be the completed restoration when the mansion would be revealed in all its 18th century glory. Jenny Cooper, by this time our official Marketing Manager, could hardly have devised a more effective strategy for promoting Moggerhanger Park in its Grade One listed status.

By this time, Jenny had trained a small army of about 50 House Tour guides, who took their turns on a rota, to cope with the large numbers of the public who wanted to see over the Main House. Guided tours were on offer every day both morning and afternoon and each day presented 'Kingdom opportunities' for sharing the faith. If ever we needed confirmation that the Lord had brought us to Moggerhanger Park, it was here to be seen.

The new 'Friends of Moggerhanger Park' newssheet, an excellent two-colour A4 paper, a more professional successor to the A5 bulletin circulated from the early days, was now being produced and regularly circulated containing not only news, thanks, and forthcoming events, but also photos and special offers for joining a circulation list of supporters.

Forward Planning for the Opening

Early in the summer of 2003, the MHPT trustees had already reviewed the progress of the work in consultation with their professional team and Bowman's management (the main contractor). Nearly two years had elapsed since the internal restoration contract had begun and at that time the work was deemed to be on target for completion by the end of February 2004. On the strength of this MHPT trustees had decided to set an actual date for a Grand Opening, and they planned a series of celebration events later in 2004 designed to thank all those who had contributed to the success of the project.

Although completion was expected in February 2004, a June date was ruled out in case there were any unforeseen delays. In order to play safe, it was decided to go for an autumn date just after the Annual Heritage weekend and to check if the Most Revd Dr Rowan Williams, the Archbishop of Canterbury, was still available to attend the opening. Through Cliff's personal relationship with him, he graciously accepted the diary engagement and agreed to come and give the main address on Saturday 2nd October 2004.

Not Everybody was Happy!

This invitation to the Archbishop did not go down well with one resident ministry – *Prophecy Today*. Cliff was no longer the editor of the magazine, and the new editor was David Andrew who, with his wife Agnes, was now occupying the Bungalow so he could be close at hand for the magazine although his involvement in other on-site matters was minimal. But in the January 2004 issue of Prophecy Today he had taken a hard line on Rowan's participation in the Welsh National Druid's Festival when he was Archbishop of Wales. David ensured that he had moved out of the Bungalow before the event and at that time he also relocated the magazine to his family home in Scotland. He closed *Prophecy Today* soon after this, renaming it 'Sword' while retaining the same format.

Planning Residential Ministry

In spite of this setback, hopes were high at the beginning of 2004 now that an opening date had been set. The Ministries were keen to recommence the CCM residential conference work which had been suspended since the main transfer of the office facilities from Yorkshire although CCM had needed to develop its ministry in slightly different ways since that time. They began planning a full programme of courses and conferences as well as follow-up to finally begin in October that year.

Brochures were printed, speakers and facilitators were booked, and the programme was advertised. These were planned to begin with a Pilot Course with different kinds of sessions using accommodation that they could test with prayer partners to ensure that it was all operating properly, before the full range of courses at Moggerhanger were fully opened to the public. We wanted it to be first used by our faithful supporters, some of whom had been among those who had contributed to the original appeal that had raised the half million pounds to secure the acquisition of the house from the developers. They had been looking forward for many years to the beginning of residential ministry at Moggerhanger.

We had had no difficulty in filling the places and taking deposits from those who were keen to be among the first residents in the House since the Hospital closed in 1987, and to celebrate the end of the long restoration period. We told all those who registered that, as they were the first to try out the restored facilities, they would be expected to help with 'snagging' by reporting anything that was not quite up to standard.

Further Delays and their Effects

We had expected the inevitability of minor delays and as already noted, the end of February 2004 came, and the work was still not finished. The contractors said that they had encountered more complications than anticipated and that the work would not now be finished until the end of May that year. We were disappointed by this, but we congratulated ourselves on having had the foresight to delay the opening date until October with the pilot courses to follow almost immediately.

In the event, when time pressed on our attempts to get things fully operational, it was not just these pilot courses being offered which we had to adapt. The printed Advent 2004 Programme contained details of several new and continuing day events like prayer mornings, 'Martha's Days Out' and Monthly Consultations on different subjects - but also many overnight, 2 day and 3-day conferences, workshops, 'State of the Nation' debates, and specialist courses. Then we had to face the fact that the Ministry actual use may be delayed for some time to come, so that only certain one-day events would be easy to hold – and they would develop along different lines. But more of that in a later volume.

Dry Rot Discovered

We watched the continuing work with growing anxiety over the next few months and then, just when we felt that it was 'all systems go', once again we were shaken as in June some of the workmen noticed fungus growing in one of the downstairs rooms next to the main entrance.

This immediately rang alarm bells, and the architects ordered a full investigation with plaster being stripped and floorboards lifted around the area. **Two rooms on the ground floor and one on the first floor were already badly affected by dry rot.**

The Trustees were dismayed to receive the report from the architects and surveyors of the extent of the infection and its cause. A rainwater gully over the main entrance was defective. It had been pouring rainwater into the hopper which had splashed back and penetrated underneath the asphalt covering on the flat roof and had caused the whole wall to become saturated. This must have taken place over a prolonged period with the result that the dry rot was now spreading rapidly. Immediate remedial action was taken and there followed what seemed to be a long period of investigation and negotiation to establish responsibility and to persuade the insurance company of one or other of the professional teams to pay for the remedial work.

Mediation Needed

It was in fact just a month later in early July 2004 when an independent surveyor's report pointed to a design fault which was immediately disputed. But on the very day that we received the report, one of our Ministry supporters, Danny Stupple, called at Moggerhanger unexpectedly as he was in the neighbourhood. He was a structural survey consultant who had been presiding at a tribunal in Bedford and having collected some past copies of *Prophecy Today*, he explained over a cup of coffee that he was an adjudicator in disputes involving professionals in the building industry!

You can imagine that it was not long before we had explained the difficulty and dispute presently facing us and he generously offered to undertake, free of charge, all the responsibility for negotiation including dealing with the insurance company who predictably proved very reluctant to admit any liability. Once again, God had intervened in the Moggerhanger story and supplied our needs in a time of crisis. We all gave thanks that Danny was the Lord's provision – another of the Moggerhanger miracles. In the event, the negotiations took nearly a year to complete, but eventually they came to a successful amicable conclusion, although we did lose the services of Mark, our long term architect

Effects of the Mediation

The discovery of dry rot and subsequent actions also meant a number of other significant things.

Having set this mediation under way to allocate responsibility and recover as much funding as possible, the Trustees decided not to replace the asphalt covering on the flat roof, but to replace it with lead in conformity with Soane's original plans. Once again costs were increased, more money was needed, and further delays were inevitable. Balancing original plans with more modern technology was always going to be a problem!

Additionally, once again, almost inevitably grant money given for creating the 'Ministry Centre' was diverted and used on the immediate needs of the house.

A subsequent action that had another immediate effect which was not recognised fully at the time, but which would become more evident later, was the probable inevitability that the needs of the Ministries, who could have guaranteed its future use, were no longer the prime reason for any action. The restoration of a Grade 1 listed house became the dominant objective, and the needs of a Ministry Centre, for which the house had been given, were often not even taken into consideration – they faded into the background where they would quietly die. Even those with prophetic insight were overwhelmed into silence.

Renaming October 2004 as the 'Spiritual' Celebration

But this late discovery of dry rot over the main entrance was also decisive in convincing the MHPT Trustees that we could not hold the 'Grand Opening Celebration' as originally booked to be held on 2nd October 2004 and the other 'thank you' parties would also need to be delayed.

A large number of different events had already been planned some of which could reasonably be put on hold including the starting of Ministry Courses and snagging which were part of the Ministries contribution. The Archbishop of Canterbury had agreed to come on that date and already a considerable amount of publicity had gone out which it would have been difficult to cancel. Two books were on target for publication. Monica had been researching the Christian roots of the Thornton family who used to live in the house, and she had written a booklet *Thornton Family Prayers* which, when residential accommodation did eventually become available, would be placed in all the bedrooms and Cliff's book on *The Wilberforce Connection* was also due to be published around that time.

In facing the inevitable delay in holding the official house opening ceremony, the Ministries at this incredibly short notice, then came to the rescue, as they had done before when the need was great. MHPT Trustees gladly handed over complete responsibility for the day to the Ministries – with the understanding that an official opening would need to be delayed once again indefinitely.

The Ministries Accept the Challenge

The Ministries knew that there would now be limited access to the Main House and that the more official opening ceremony would need to have alternative plans. Having come this far, they were growing used to last-minute setbacks and challenges to 'think outside the box'. They were not overly disheartened or willing to accept any form of defeat – there must be another way! They offered to make the day what they called 'A Spiritual Opening' and a catalyst for a 'movement for change' in the moral and spiritual values of the nation.

The combined Ministries 2003 'Open Day' which had been held on 18th October the previous year had taken as its theme 'the heritage of the Thornton and Wilberforce families'. It was agreed that this same theme would be expanded this year into a celebration of the 'Spiritual Heritage of the House' and the day came to be known as the 'Spiritual Opening of Moggerhanger Park'.

Change of Emphasis

Peter Inskip had always put the best possible restoration of the building first and foremost – he maintained that 'the building will be here long after you Christians have gone'. We wanted to be good stewards, but we knew that ministry is NOT dependent on buildings. Donald McGavran, one of the founding fathers of the Church Growth Movement, used to say that buildings are not essential for Christian mission although they have their use – especially when it's raining! He said that "*the church has to be, and will be seen as, the **people** of that time*' and we had occasion to continually recall this message as we finalised plans.

We therefore saw the 'Spiritual Opening' as the opportunity to celebrate the lives of those who had been associated with the House who were an important part of its heritage. We did not want the event just to celebrate a Mausoleum or to adulate a famous architect. It was the **faith and mission** of those who had been connected with the building that was important. These were the spiritual heritage and that legacy that it was important to leave for the next generation.

The Spiritual Heritage Celebration of Moggerhanger Park was expected to provide an opportunity to build on this legacy so that there would be a good foundation for when the Main House itself did at last become fully operational. At that stage we did not know that this was fast becoming a dream that would not be fulfilled in our time. Despite all the problems we continued in hope, and we threw all our energies and resources into a day of celebration – giving thanks to God for the great spiritual heritage of the house which we were convinced would one day be its central focus.

The pre-publicity and the Programme for The Day stated:

> Although the restoration of the House has not yet been completed, there is much to rejoice in, and we welcome a number of distinguished guests to share this time of spiritual celebration with us . . . Today we recognise with thanksgiving the spiritual heritage of Moggerhanger House and the goodness of God in entrusting the House to the stewardship of the Trustees and Directors who share the responsibility for the House, the estate, and its future use. In so doing we affirm our commitment to using the House in such a way that it will fulfil the vision God gave to us in bringing us here and it will bring glory to the name of the Lord Jesus Christ.

Chapter Twelve
CELEBRATING THE SPIRITUAL HERITAGE

A generous gift of marquees encourages the team in their preparations for the great event. The details of the day are described in this chapter which includes a tour of the house for the 500 who spend the day at Moggerhanger Park. The Archbishop of Canterbury dedicates the Chapel in the House as one of the highlights of the day celebrating its spiritual heritage.

By the time any decision over dates and action had finally been made, and the challenge had been accepted, there was now fewer than five months before the event to make the changes necessary, postpone as long as possible the courses due to signal that the House was open for activity, and to agree an appropriate programme for this day that would then need to fulfil a new set of expectations. There was no budget available, and we needed to draw on our experience, existing volunteers, and staff – but there was great determination and goodwill. Computers were humming, telephones never stopped ringing – it was all hands to the mill.

We knew there would be no cutting of a ribbon and then all moving into the Main House to take in its restored beauty – although we were planning on giving limited guided tours and highlighting what we could of this Soane masterpiece. We would indeed be limited in even being able to show off the more recent addition of the woods and grounds – although in this case, we would encourage exploration and have much literature available to supplement both aspects. But our emphasis now would need to be almost entirely on what the Ministries could do to help publicise the House and estate so that it could become an influence in the land and build on the Thornton and Clapham links from the past.

So, the planning of the content of what we agreed should be an all-day event for those who came, should be the priority – and, if possible, we should even be offering samples of the kind of courses we could hold and how the house would be used. The theme we took was one which was becoming increasingly familiar – 'A 21st Century Clapham Initiative'.

The Gift

It is wonderful how the Lord supplies all our needs even in times of hardship and difficulty. We now would have no accommodation at Moggerhanger Park to offer for visitors travelling a distance or wishing to stay overnight, and nowhere even to host a large day-time event such as we were now planning for the October House Spiritual Opening Celebration. On hearing on the grapevine of our changed circumstances, some dear friends in Devon came to our rescue with an offer of marquees – free of charge as a gift to our ministry.

Marquees from Devon

Malcolm and Christine Ford owned a farm, Rora House, in beautiful Devon countryside near Newton Abbott, which they used for ministry. We had been there many times and spoken to their community. The farmhouse had been enlarged to provide bedrooms for visitors and a large worship centre had also been added. But throughout the summer months they held large gatherings for a succession of Bible weeks for which they used their barns and erected their own large marquees in the fields. They particularly specialised in children's events and family gatherings.

Their season finished in September, and as we had earlier in the year moved our celebration to October, they offered their marquees to us for this event completely free of charge including delivery. They sent two large marquees and a third of an even greater giant size, seating several hundred. These were all loaded onto transporters, together with over 500 folding chairs, and driven from Devon to Moggerhanger together with a team to carry out the erection of the marquees which was quite a specialised task in itself. The team remained for the weekend and joined in the celebrations, before dismantling the marquees and taking them back to Devonshire. All this was an amazing free gift from our friends and opened up more doors to further possibilities for the future.

Site Planning and More Offers

The largest Marquee was given pride of place on the back lawn in full view of the House, and this was where the main events planned for the day would take place. Staging was offered by a local supporting group, matting was offered by another local professional supporter who had caught the vision, as had two different groups with sound and recording equipment and the skills and ability needed to go with it. Even the beautiful floral decorations throughout the marquee, some of which would figure dramatically later in the day, were given by a local florist who continued to supply the House with flowers for many more years once it finally did open. So everything was supplied by our friends who wanted to be a part of this great celebration, free of charge.

We also had a 'Book Stall' in one corner and a clearly marked 'First Aid Point' in another staffed by Sally Fawkes. She had been involved with the community since the start and was now living in the village and was also a State Registered Nurse. The Lord had already given us so many of the resources and skills that we would need.

We were grateful for the extensive back lawn which, ever since the removal of the hospital wards ten years or so ago, had already proved its worth on many occasions and was well maintained. One of the marquees was used as an exhibition centre where the work of each of the Moggerhanger Ministries was displayed with staff available to talk about their ministry and even give scheduled seminars on different aspects at advertised times. Monica's new booklet the *'Thornton Family Prayers'* was available, and Cliff had a table for signing his new book *'The Wilberforce Connection'*. The remaining marquee, rather smaller, was used as a 'Speakers Marquee' and rallying point. It also served well for the coordination of the complex programme.

The Garden Room, alongside the Stable-block offices was used entirely for refreshments where full meals were served with many volunteer waiters. Some minor culinary miracles took place in the small Garden Room kitchen presided over by Jim Fitzgerald who was to become the chef in charge of the Moggerhanger Park restaurant in the future. There were numerous further tea and coffee points set up around the site.

Who to Invite?

It was agreed from the start that we would need a large team of volunteer helpers and this could not be an open event but would need to be 'by invitation only'. These invitations would need to go out with a covering letter well in advance – or at least as soon as we could. Building the invitation list was one of the keys to the event – and to ensure that no-one was missing. Each of the Ministries supplied more volunteers and gathered other names and circulated the information: it was a 'ticket only' event and the 500 reserved spaces available soon filled – and as many again became directly involved and took part in some way or another.

Looking to the Future

We tried to cover every eventuality and also give a foretaste of what was still to come. We were not making any charge for admission, so we launched two funds to be initiated on the day – 'A House Opening Fund' with special forms, which had a specially promoted area on the C&M Ministries stand in the Exhibition centre. The collection at the main afternoon event was made over to the Ministries special 'Wilberforce Fund' to cover the costs of the day and to be used for establishing new Ministries to come out of, and be linked with, Moggerhanger.

A full programme appeared in the 'Welcome Pack' which also had a full plan of the site on the back so that no-one could get lost! Most may have already visited at least once and there was a whole page of pictures of the House and events during the last ten years for them to recognise. There were also many first-time newcomers who had not visited before and might not have been fully aware of what to expect. We had to adapt events for the occasion so as to include many options for involvement and experiences in a varied programme for a full day.

The Day of Celebration and Thanksgiving

Some 500 invited guests, who had all received individual invitations from names submitted by the ten Ministries now involved, attended the full day event (from 10.00 am to 5.30 pm) on Saturday 2nd October 2004 which 'praise the Lord' was fine and clear with sunshine for most of the day. Teams of Community Volunteers, Staff and Trustees carried responsibility for everything from welcoming and parking to catering, guiding, and exhibitions. The organisational activity for the preparation work required, needed a team of its own all working closely together – and linked by mobile phones – where possible!

Everyone had received a copy of the 24 page A4 glossy Souvenir Programme at the Welcome Desk by the cattle grid at the estate entrance, with all the information it was expected that they would need and also giving details of all these coordinating ministries who were displaying in the exhibition tent. Information was given of the four sessions in the Main Marquee as well as several further options for participation including refreshments, and the timed tours of the House, grounds, and visits to the Offices with arrangements for signing up for these.

The site plan on the back of the programme was much appreciated as were the Special Badges which had been prepared for the Team, Guides and Trustees so that they were easily identifiable to answer further questions. All had been primed with answers - or at least knew who they could turn to for help. The Teamwork seemed to be working like clockwork!

A Varied and Exciting Programme

There were always various activities going on at the same time, and no compulsory programme. The Garden Room was serving refreshments from the start, the Exhibition Hall and various information centres were open throughout the day, flexibly helping visitors to make the most of the experience.

Morning Prayers: The day began at 10.00 am with as many of the helpers who could be spared, plus the earliest arrivals, gathering for 'Victorian Morning Prayers' in the central marquee, in the same way as we imagined they would have been held in the House in its heyday. We sang an Isaac Watts hymn '*Come let us join our cheerful songs*' and Rev Gillian Orpin, our recently appointed Chaplain to the community, read from Hebrews 11 the lovely passage on Faith. Monica closed this short committal of the day with one of the prayers by Henry Thornton taken from the collection of prayers in her '*Thornton Family Prayers*' which would be officially launched during the lunch hour.

Joyful worship took place at various occasions during the day and was led throughout by a music group from Bromham Baptist Church. This group was led by Andrew and Marion Ingrey-Senn who had been part of the community of believers planning the Moggerhanger project from the early days, several years before we discovered Moggerhanger Park.

Slavery - Past and Present: Following the 10 am Morning Prayers, the next session in the main Marquee followed at 11.00 am and built on the influence of the Clapham Group led by the Clapham Thorntons and William Wilberforce in the late 18th and early 19th centuries. This is still recognised today and is especially remembered in Westminster where MPs of all parties regard Wilberforce's example as one of the treasures of Parliamentary history. It was appropriate that this day of celebration at Moggerhanger Park should include reference to Wilberforce and the Clapham Group.

The Walk: This second session started with a monologue given by Andrew Harrison 'The Walk', written by Murray Watts. This was a dramatic presentation of William Wilberforce's life-changing encounter with John Newton, the former slave-ship owner turned evangelical preacher. It was this encounter at a critical point in Wilberforce's life that determined his future. He was struggling with the decision on whether to enter the church as a preacher or to continue in politics and make his life's ambition the abolition of slavery.

This monologue on the life and times of Wilberforce and the abolition of the slave trade had become a major feature in the public meetings being undertaken by the CCM team. It had already been performed in many venues around the country. It was therefore appropriate that it should be presented here on this special day in the life of our Ministry base, with its historic connections with the Wilberforce and Thornton families. A repeat performance was also given later in the day.

Slavery Today: Our next speaker had been a friend of Family Matters Institute for many years and one of their Trustees, being actively involved in their research as well as having links with Parliament. Dr Carrie Pemberton, CEO of 'The Churches Alert to Sex Trafficking Across Europe' (CHASTE) described the extent of a current little known problems today – that of people-trafficking as a modern form of slavery. Carrie was horrified at the extent of the slave trade in Europe today that was attracting criminals from the Far East. They were promising careers with training, to girls from poor countries who were then virtually being sold into slavery and transported to Europe and ending up in brothels. She was alerting churches to the extent of this evil, and trying to mobilise Christian opinion to seek stronger action against the trade. She thanked Dr Williams for the support that he had already given to her campaign.

The Wilberforce Connection Book Launch: Tony Collins, Editorial Director of Monarch Books, then spoke about the importance of Cliff's new book on the Eighteenth-Century work of the Clapham Group and their continuing significance for today.

During the lunchbreak that followed, book signing sessions were held for both *The Wilberforce Connection* and *The Thornton Family Prayers*.

House Tours: Of the 500 people attending that day, most were able to book onto conducted tours of the House to see the progress of the restoration at different times during the day. The Construction Restoration Team had been very cooperative in ensuring that everything was safe, and we knew the areas that would be closed off and inaccessible. Short tours of the grounds were also organised using volunteer guides to take parties around the Walled Gardens, the Icehouse and woods, as well as to see the outside of the house and its main architectural features.

The only major difficulty was that there were only four toilets available for 500 people! There were two attached to the Garden Room that were kept for the ladies and the two in the Stable Courtyard offices were kept for the men. Inevitably there were long queues and we offered to take the Archbishop up to the empty Bungalow at lunchtime, but he insisted on queueing with the men where he could enjoy informal conversation with those around him. We were quite impressed with his humility.

Dedicating the Chapel: During the lunch break from the main activities in the large Marquee, the Archbishop was given a special tour of the House with the MHPT Trustees, and when we reached the room that had once been Mrs Thornton's boudoir on the first floor, we explained to the Archbishop that this was now being restored as a chapel. We had previously notified him of our intention to ask him if he would be kind enough to dedicate the room for its future use as a chapel for the Community. The Archbishop had kindly agreed to this and in the presence of the Trustees of Harvest Vision and MHPT, and the Reverend Gillian Orpin, who was becoming more active as Chaplain to the Community, he stood and dedicated the room in prayer.

That room would later be used, not only for community prayer times, but also as the scene where many couples with links to our growing Community made their marriage vows and received the blessing of the presence of the Lord. It was during the next phase that the Community would have this as its own chapel base and be able to perform its own weddings – but more about that in the next volume.

The Main Celebration of the Spiritual Heritage

The afternoon between 2 and 4 pm was given over to being the main united celebration event of the day with a number of definable parts with many members of the wider Ministry Community taking part – Revd Dr John Job, chair of CCM which was now the main Ministry on the site, led prayers; Mr Andrew Ingrey-Senn, chairman of Harvest Vision spoke of the Vision; Mrs Jenny Forbes, a past Trustee and valued member of PWM and now fully involved in Pardes at Moggerhanger and a leader in the Lydia Prayer Fellowship, gave the prayers of thanksgiving, confession and intercession, and Sir Sam Whitbread, chair of MHPT, read the Scriptures. Among other visiting supporters also taking part was one of our local MPs, Alistair Burt, who was also Chair of the All-Party Christian Fellowship in Parliament. He had brought greetings from Westminster early in the afternoon.

Monica welcomed everybody to Moggerhanger Park for the Main session of this celebration and after a time of worship and John Job's prayer of invocation, she introduced all the different Ministries after which Andrew Ingrey-Senn communicated the Vision, being joined in this by Cliff and Monica. Together they spoke of the early days of searching for the right place in fulfilment of the promise God had made many years earlier that he would give a place for prayer and study where many could come for spiritual refreshment. It had always been intended that people with leadership responsibilities would come to spend time seeking the Lord for guidance and strength and this continued to be one of the main objectives.

They briefly described the journey that had brought them to this day: the formation of a 'Community of Believers' who were at the heart of the Moggerhanger project and the time they had spent in prayer seeking for this place, They then went on to describe how they had found Moggerhanger Park, the condition of the buildings and the promises that God had made that the proposed houses surrounding the House would never be built. They gave thanks for the wonderful way in which God had fulfilled his promises and although many problems had been encountered along the way, now there was great hope that, despite the delays, we were in sight of the days when the House would be used as the Ministry Centre that was the original vision.

Britain Today – An African View

The next session took a different perspective and Cliff introduced Pastor Wale Babatunde, an African preacher with whom we had been friends for many years. It was expected that many immigrant communities, from both Africa and the West Indies would find their home at the Moggerhanger of the future. In his introduction, Cliff spoke about how he and Monica had been to Nigeria on a number of occasions, and how they had become friends with Solomon and Mary Lar and how Mary had stayed in the Gatehouse at Moggerhanger Park where she had written an autobiographical book that Monica had edited and published for her. Cliff spoke highly of the work of Nigerian-led churches in Britain and how he had spoken at Wale's church in South London, and he was glad to welcome Wale to Moggerhanger Park.

Wale Babatunde then spoke of his shock in coming to Britain and discovering that it was not the godly society that he had expected to encounter. He described his earlier life in Africa and how much he had benefited from Christian missionaries in his early education. It was English Christians who had not only taken the gospel to Nigeria but had established schools and administrative facilities as well as physical things such as roads and electricity supplies. He said that his nation had a great regard for Britain and the godly heritage that they had implanted. It was therefore a huge shock to him to discover that in England the churches were not full on Sundays and there was a lack of respect for the gospel.

Sam Whitbread, as Chair of MHPT, showed their support of all that the Ministries were doing today by reading the wonderful passage of encouragement in Isaiah 61.v 1-4. Cliff followed this with an outline of what he believed was the word from the Lord for Britain today.

Archbishop Williams on the Clapham Sect

Archbishop Rowan Williams was the guest of honour at this day, and he was warmly welcomed by Cliff who spoke of their friendship which went back to the time when Rowan had been Archbishop of the Church in Wales.

Rowan began by expressing his own personal admiration for the work of William Wilberforce and the monumental influence of the Clapham Sect and their work in transforming 18th Century society. This was not simply due to political philosophy but was an expression of their evangelical faith in God.

He offered a comparative study of social and spiritual conditions in 18th century Britain which was the background to the work of Wilberforce and the Christian group of reformers that he had led. He could see many similarities with our situation today and declared that there is a great need for a similar commitment to a biblical gospel of transformation today. He said that there were plenty of people in the 18th-century who had opposed slavery on humanitarian grounds stemming from the enlightenment, but the difference with the Clapham Group was their Christian commitment. They were committed to change society – but they also knew that it was only God who could change human beings. Each of them had that personal conviction because they knew that God had changed them.

Rowan then spoke about Hannah More, one of the Clapham Group, who worked among the poor helping them to read and write. But she also spoke to the rich, the secure, and the prosperous, of their obligation to their fellow human beings who did not have their advantages. She urged them to share a sense of mutual obligation, of debt and duty to others.

The Archbishop reminded us that we owe everything to God. He said that the great social and international vision of the Clapham Group, all that they were and all that they had, had come from God and we have an eternal debt to God. As God had transformed us, so we should be committed to transforming the lives of others in the world that we so often blaspheme and distort by our greed and our manipulation.

The Power of the Spirit

His speech was interrupted by a powerful gust of wind that swept through the open vent at the front of the marquee sending a large vase of flowers tumbling across the stage with a noisy clatter. It startled everyone in the marquee and there was a moment of dramatic silence.

It was almost as though it was stage-managed for the Archbishop, who made good use of it by describing it as a symbol of the power of the Holy Spirit that filled and transformed the lives of the disciples on the Day of Pentecost. He spoke of the divine energy that empowered the disciples to go out onto the streets of Jerusalem and to declare the gospel of the Risen Jesus. And it was this same power of the Holy Spirit that was available to us today and it was the only means by which the nation was going to be transformed.

Rowan reminded us that the disciples were able to do nothing in their own strength, but they were entirely reliant upon the power of the Spirit of God. The strong wind blowing through the marquee was certainly seen as an encouraging sign by all those listening to the Archbishop. It also enriched the spirit of worship and increased an awareness of the presence of the Lord for all who were worshipping in the marquee on that day of celebration.

Prayer and Worship

This incident of the powerful wind was followed by a time of intercessory prayer led by the Rt Revd Richard Inwood, Bishop of Bedford as part of the worship. It was certainly enriched by what we all saw as the wind of the Holy Spirit blowing across Moggerhanger Park. It seemed to be a demonstration of the presence of the Lord, the God of Creation, and the affirmation of his presence at Moggerhanger Park and his blessing upon the Ministry Centre that was at the heart of the whole Moggerhanger project and the reason it had been given by God and entrusted to our keeping.

The time of prayer was followed by the singing of the hymn: 'These are the days of Elijah' which added to the sense of expectation and looking confidently to the future in the belief that God was going to bless the future work at Moggerhanger Park, provided, of course, that we put our trust entirely in him, recognising, as the Archbishop had said, that we can do nothing in our own strength.

Looking Forward

After a further break for chances to explore the grounds more, sign the Visitors Book, go on further tours, ask questions, browse in the exhibition, or enjoy more cake, tea and fellowship, the final event of the day was held in the Main Marquee

Three prominent founder/leaders in *TransformUK*, – Andrea Williams, Sally Davis, and Francis Goodwin – all of whom had been with us at the earlier Ministry Open Day in July which had built on the 2003 Open Day, gave a preview of their presentation that was just about to go on a nationwide tour; Andy Harrison gave a repeat performance of 'The Walk', the monologue from Riding Lights on Wilberforce's encounter with John Newton. And finally, Pastor Wale, and his wife Precious, Babatunde led in a moving epilogue and prayer. The day finished as it began with praising God for all his provision.

Significance

Many of those present in that Marquee at Moggerhanger Park shared in a sense of the significance of this occasion in the life of the nation. There was much discussion afterwards on the role of Moggerhanger Park as a Ministry Centre that would serve the nation in the time of great upheaval and shaking that was coming. It was recognised that this was a place that had been given as a sacred trust by God for fulfilling his good purposes for the transformation of the nation.

What Next?

In spite of all the setbacks and battles to reach this point, the Spiritual Opening was a highlight with which we will end this volume and one on which we can look back with gratitude as it raised everybody's morale – it gave us a purpose, a belief and hope in the future.

We knew this would only happen if we did not try to direct things by our own human wisdom. We were entering an unknown future that was not going to be easy but many caught a new vision, so we could move forward knowing that with our confidence in the Lord he would never forsake us.

REFLECTIONS ON THE JOURNEY
SO FAR

Looking back over these first 11 years of the modern history at Moggerhanger Park (covering the time in which the ministries were active and in possession), we give thanks to God for his presence and guidance often through very difficult situations. There were times when we had to make decisions with far-reaching consequences, when we desperately needed the wisdom of God. These were especially when others wanted us to do things their way or did not appear to understand our purposes and so put barriers in the way. We have often been in battle situations when the praying community played a major role in the final outcome.

It is astonishing to see the number of 'divine interventions' that occurred during this period when it was obvious that if we had just used our insights and been working in our human strength we would have failed. But should we have been astonished? Undoubtedly the house had been given to us by God. This was the fundamental fact at the centre of all our policy decisions. *The house was not ours; it was God's.* We were in fact just Stewards and, therefore, all decisions regarding the house had to be guided by God and to be pleasing in his sight. We knew that if we were doing things his way, he would direct the way forward. Our task was to ensure that we were rightly hearing from the Lord.

We had already discovered that we did not have the complete picture as to how this would be achieved, especially as two of the founding ministries ceased to operate within this period but the need was still there and the baton had been passed on and others took it forward. We knew we always had a reliable source to turn to when God's plans appeared to differ from our human wishes and we needed to recognise, and be able to discern, when any distraction was not of his making.

Knowing that the house belonged to God and not to us, gave us the confidence to oppose the Developers when they wanted to increase the size of the houses - for which they already had planning permission. Even when they threatened to evict us from the Bungalow and to retake Moggerhanger House from Harvest Vision, we did not waver in opposing them, because the house was not ours but God's, and we were confident that he would defend it. At that stage all the leadership team were part of the community of believers. It is interesting, looking back, that all the miracles of provision took place before the setting up of the Preservation Trust.

Modus Operandi

Two other outstanding confirmations have been in terms of the ways that we carried out leadership and community.

Our type of leadership has always been nondirective, and it was never so much WHAT we did, but HOW we did it that mattered. We had seen this operating effectively in our ministry in London. There is never only one specific way of doing things – God does not provide a Blueprint – and what works in one area will not necessarily work in another or at a different time. This means that we constantly have to seek the Lord for each new situation.

God had been preparing the way ahead before we discovered Moggerhanger Park. He had drawn together a small praying community with a shared vision. Having a common purpose meant that it made collective rather than dictated decision-making possible. This, of course, only works smoothly, and effectively in a community of believers where each one is committed to the leadership of Jesus. Micah expresses this beautifully, *"He has showed you, O man, what is good. And what does the Lord require of you? To act justly and to love mercy and to walk humbly with your God"* (Micah 6:8). It is walking humbly with the Lord God that makes the journey exciting and effective.

If there are those who do not believe in the vision in the community, this kind of leadership is despised and rejected as they will only be thinking in worldly terms. Every part of the operation is affected – divine guidance is a nonsense to the unbeliever. Therefore, trusting the Lord to provide is impossible – the unbeliever seeks assurance from banks and business deals. It is as Jesus said, impossible to serve two Masters. Paul faces the situation head-on – *"the man without the Spirit does not accept the things that come from the Spirit of God, for they are foolishness to him, and he cannot understand them, because they are spiritually discerned"* (1 Cor 2:14).

The basic trouble is that believers and unbelievers are on entirely different planes. Isaiah realised this when he heard God saying *"as the heavens are higher than the earth so are my ways higher than your ways and my thoughts than your thoughts"* (Is 55:9). This was the problem we faced at Moggerhanger Park when in order to provide the funding we needed to take people into the Preservation Trust who had a different vision and were not on the same plane as the community of believers. On the surface we all had a common objective in the restoration of the buildings, but when difficult decisions had to be made, we had entirely different methods of decision-making!

Taking Note of Warnings

We had received warnings of the difficulties in being involved in listed buildings. So, we were expecting difficulties with authorities such as English Heritage and HLF, but there were also difficulties to face **within our own team**. It was essential to both pray and to plan with a shared vision in front of us. If we were ever in times of doubt, we needed to keep a sense of realism recognising that we were part of God's overall plans in fulfilling other visions of those around us and we needed a team around us with this shared vision: and this was becoming increasingly impossible.

These were just some of the first fundamental principles underlying all our decision-making for the original Harvest Vision trustees. In times of difficult decision-making, we would stop the meeting and turn to prayer, but in MHPT this also became impossible because the unbelievers had no understanding of how to pray. They actually said that when we prayed it made them feel uncomfortable. We no longer had around us a team with a fully shared vision such as we had had in the early days of our acquisition of Moggerhanger Park.

Lateral Thinking

We often had to adapt our plans to changing circumstances and we quickly recognised that things did not, and would not, always happen smoothly and quickly – but we also realised that we had to learn to think laterally: first checking that the objective we were seeking was right and then looking for other ways in which it could be fulfilled. There would always be something we could do even when the way forward appeared blocked. In earlier days, when we had a community with a shared vision of hope and trust in God, we could accept and rejoice whatever the circumstances. In this way our vision was continually being widened, as we were often taken along an unexpected road.

When we set up Moggerhanger House Preservation Trust (MHPT) everything changed. Until that point our objective was quite simply to establish a Ministry Centre – a homebase for our ministries. All we required was good sound functional buildings that would provide conference facilities for about 30 people – bedrooms and lecture rooms and, of course dining rooms. Moggerhanger House together with its Stable Courtyard buildings was an ideal size to meet our requirements. The buildings simply had to be adapted to provide the facilities that were required by the ministry.

At that time, we had about 4000 ministry supporters and an abundance of voluntary helpers. All we needed was expert architects to design the changes needed in the buildings and tradesmen to carry out the physical work that could not be achieved by volunteers. The intervention of English Heritage and the upgrading of the house to Grade One forced us to change our perspectives. This was something quite unforeseen, but we concluded that God is never taken by surprise. He obviously knew what was going to happen. Nevertheless, he had brought us here to Moggerhanger Park. That was an established fact that had been proven by events where the hand of God was clearly seen.

Widening the Vision

In the light of these major changes, we had made a major policy change – from adapting the buildings to accommodate our ministry needs, to adjusting our ministry needs to fit in with the accommodation provided by Moggerhanger Park – which had been given to us by God. We could not despise this precious gift of God that we found others were valuing too as the heritage of the nation, we had to find ways of using it expressly for the advancement of the Kingdom of God. We found the answer to this in the spiritual heritage of the house – its historic links with the Clapham Sect led by William Wilberforce, first cousin of Godfrey Thornton, the owner of the house in the latter part of the 18th century.

Our study of the work of the Clapham Group of social reformers showed strong links with the work of social transformation that was a central objective of the ministries that we bought to Moggerhanger Park. Surely, we reasoned, this is why God has brought us to this place, therefore we have to do whatever is necessary to fulfil God's purpose in bringing us here.

We were offered a grant of £3 million from public funds to restore the house because of its value to the nation. We recognised that this would bring people from far and wide to see the architectural value of the house. This value combined with the historical links to the Clapham Group could be used for the Kingdom. People would be coming to us and we could share our faith with them simply by referring to the history of the house and relating that to the sociocultural needs of today. It was a brilliant strategy that gave us great hope for the future.

When 'The Observer', a national Sunday newspaper, devoted four pages to the newly discovered architectural treasures of Sir John Soane's work, this brought some 3000 people to visit Moggerhanger Park the following weekend. Most of those visitors asked two questions: "Who used to live here?" and "What are you doing with it now?" This gave us the ideal opportunity of sharing our faith with members of the public which inevitably strengthened our belief that God had brought us here knowing that it was going to be upgraded to Grade 1. Therefore, we had to be flexible to achieve the objective of establishing a Ministry Centre while at the same time restoring a national architectural treasure.

This was why we gladly submitted to establishing a Preservation Trust some of whose trustees would have special qualifications for carrying out the restoration work, but they would not necessarily be Bible believing Christians. We had to accept this and now find ways of working with a mixed group of Trustees in order to fulfil our ministry objectives. Of course, it was difficult but this was the task we believed that God had called us to fulfil. It was made much more difficult by the loss of several strong Christians by death or removal from the area.

Learning and Adapting

One of the major difficulties we faced in MHPT was with the newly created Heritage Lottery Fund (HLF), not known to have any Christian links and whose staff had no experience of restoring a Grade 1 listed property and in the opinion of our professional team they behaved very poorly. This created enormous bureaucratic delays which increased costs and created financial problems. We were constantly seeking funds from other sources. In addition, we discovered dry rot which further increased costs and then (read the next volume) a beam in the 'Eating Room' sagged causing the whole of the two floors above to be unusable and created more delays in restoring the buildings.

Despite the differences within the MHPT trustees all these difficulties encountered were dealt with while maintaining unity. When dry rot and the discovery of an ancient well in the lower ground floor caused the official opening to be postponed, the ministries came to the rescue by turning the postponed event into a celebration of the spiritual heritage of the house. This turning of misfortune into blessing was a demonstration of the Kingdom principles upon which the ministries were working which makes a fitting climax to the record of the story thus far.

We were on a strong learning curve. Much prayer was needed and often seemed to be the only answer when our ability as Christians, no matter how well qualified, to operate and sustain commercial operations was questioned and challenged. We learned how to work as a team to deal with tensions whether inside or outside our own vision.

We knew that any effective Ministry needed a clear sense of purpose, and while it would benefit from an actual base, it could thrive even without good buildings and that relationships were of even greater importance. The restoration of a graded building was always going to be expensive and however much money we raised, more would be needed, and it would readily eat up all resources available.

The delays were already meaning that we were depending on the Lord to oversee any changes in policy to adapt our Ministry to operate in the buildings that were available to us at the time.

Ironically as our responsibilities for the house grew, so did those of the Ministries - and their supporters cooperated well and thrived in working together.

Being with or without money caused problems and fresh financial grants coming in brought both blessings and further problems - but NHMF offering us a large grant to cover greater expenses had indeed been a mixed blessing.

Cooperation important to Moving Forward

Although we appeared to have won one battle, the nature of the battle had changed when the new firm of developers wanted enhanced housing, fear and compromise threatened but powerful believing prayer prevailed. Although devious means had been used, we received very welcome support at County level which was to stand us in good stead in the future.

We learned that standing still was not an option as it would inevitably lead to decline, but to move forward would never be smooth. Solving one problem always seemed to raise many more (often coming with conditions) – more miracles were needed and our alertness, watchfulness and understanding grew as we saw the hand of God. By cooperation with others like the Council and past parliamentarians to whom we had proved our competence, we were able to deal with specific issues without too much compromise and sticking to principles brought results.

Forming new Trusts with specific objectives and support groups became the norm – ensuring good relationships continued to prevail as much as possible – more on a

Commonwealth than Empire model – but establishing new traditions with all those advantages. We needed to ensure that every group also had a 'Business Plan' which would need to be constantly revised.

Building in Long Term Sustainability

We had to prove ourselves in many areas in which we personally had little expertise, particularly against mistrust and we learned to accept gratefully the services of those who were at the centre of the battles while also understanding their need to hand on to others waiting in the wings to take it to the next stage. Teamwork and trust were so important.

We had to recognise the inevitability of change and the need for sustainability when life-changing internal events took place in the Ministry that were not just caused by the slow pace of the restoration. Vision and mission objectives COULD be maintained, the remit could be extended and that 'going out' with the message was a preparation for bringing others in.

We were involved for the long haul and anything worthwhile could not be rushed. This was one of the major lessons we needed to learn alongside thinking laterally which enabled us to set up an even more long-term event in the Spiritual Opening with which this volume ends. Celebrating in this way gave us faith for the future with even wider objectives that would indeed enable the house once again to be a voice to the nation.

Being Prepared for the Unexpected

Although we had already been involved at Moggerhanger for 11 years and would be for a similar number to come, we were totally unaware that we would never actually see the Ministry Centre completed. Even so large numbers of people came to benefit from the great deal of biblical, Hebraic and Kingdom teaching given using the space that WAS available and they were enjoying the fellowship with other Christian believers that they found at Moggerhanger Park. The value of this community work is beyond evaluation. For many people it was a life-changing experience as many of their recorded memories bear testimony on our website.

One plus factor was the wide nature of the vision that was caught by a large number who became involved with every individual being valued and having something to give which could either enable or hinder the way forward.

Another plus factor which was becoming obvious was that a multiplicity of ministries brings in new people with fresh interests and new ideas. Changes must take place as the social scene changes and also with each generation and group even though the underlying principles need to be identified and remain the same.

Every building has a past which can be built upon - but this should always be done positively and be able to have some relevance to today's society to have any impact.

This Part One Volume clearly demonstrates the great potential of Moggerhanger House for fulfilling at least some of the purposes for which it was founded and used over the years while making an impact upon the national scene. It also demonstrates the financial viability of Moggerhanger Park when it is operated in accordance with the original vision.

The review of events we have recorded in this book from 1993 to 2004 are, of course, not the end of the story – there is much more to come, some of which we have already written up in Part Two of the Moggerhanger Chronicles. We aim to publish this very soon after this first volume appears. It also demonstrates not only the power of the hand of God in blessing the work of those who put their trust in him and follow the vision that he provides, but also what happens when people put trust in themselves and fail to follow the vision he has provided!

A VISUAL PRESENTATION

SURVEYING THE TASK IN 1993 [CHAPTER 1, PAGE 11]

PRAYER PARTNERS GIVING THANKS ON THE BACK LAWN, 1994
[CHAPTER 2, PAGES 30-31]

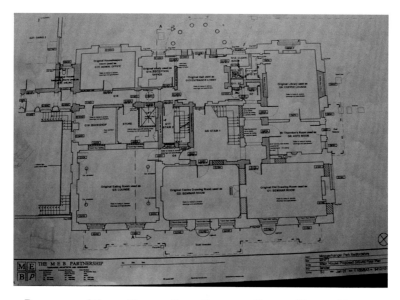

Planning What Could Be – Ground Floor House Plans
[chapter 2, pages 22-23, 35]

Protecting the Main House – Restoration Starts 1996
[chapter 3, page 57]

GREAT FIGURES IN THE PAST [CHAPTERS 3,11; PAGES 48, 159]:
GODFREY THORNTON, HUMPHRY REPTON [TOP LEFT & RIGHT]
JOHN SOANE [MIDDLE]
STEPHEN THORNTON, WILLIAM WILBERFORCE [BOTTOM LEFT & RIGHT]

THE ALL-IMPORTANT EATING ROOM
[CHAPTER 2, PAGE 36]

WORKING PARTY LUNCHTME 1994
[CHAPTERS 2, 3; PAGES 30, 42]

PAINTING THE OFFICES FOR PWM 1996
[CHAPTER 3, PAGE 52]

GATEHOUSE POTENTIAL
[CHAPTER 3, PAGE 43]

WARD 6 – THE GARDEN ROOM AND EVENTS BASE
[CHAPTERS 2, 10; PAGES 36, 136]

BLUEBELLS IN THE WOODS
[CHAPTER 11, PAGE 157]

A VISUAL PRESENTATION

TEACHING DAYS IN THE GARDEN ROOM
[CHAPTER 2, PAGE 36]

SYMBOLIC 200 YEAR OLD COPPER BEECH
[CHAPTER 10, PAGE 140]

AERIAL VIEW IN 2000

MARQUEE ACCOMMODATION FOR SPECIAL EVENTS
[CHAPTER 7, PAGE 102]